MAN, The Spiritual

MAN, The Spiritual

An Intercultural Expansion of Swami Vivekananda's Synthetic Vision of Humanity

Volume - II

Santi Nath Chattopadhyay

GYAN

First Published, 2017

Published by

Gyan Publishing House
5, Ansari Road
Daryaganj, New Delhi-110002
Phone: 9811692060
E-mail: books@gyanbooks.com

Printed at: G. Print Process, Delhi.

Cataloging in Publication Data—DK
Courtesy: D.K. Agencies (P) Ltd. <docinfo@dkagencies.com>

Chattopadhyay, Santinath, author.
Man, the spiritual : an intercultural expansion of Swami Vivekananda's synthetic vision of humanity / Santi Nath Chattopadhyay.
pages cm
Includes bibliographical references.
ISBN 9788121213530

1. Vivekananda, Swami, 1863-1902. 2. Philosophical anthropology. 3. Humanism. I. Title.

B5134.V58C43 2017 DDC 144 23

Contents

Dedicated to

Swami Vivekananda,

In Commemoration of his 150th Birth Anniversary

Preface

The present work aims at discussing the position and prospect of developing Man in the context of critical and comparative analysis of the Indian and Western Philosophical, Religious and Socio-cultural perspective as visualised by Swami Vivekananda.

The treatise seeks to present an evaluation of the transcendent–experiential states of human existence which lead to the development of the Philosophy of Man, The Spiritual. In examining Swamiji's view of Man, it may be stated that it is not mere a concept or doctrine but on the other hand it is the manifestation of human potentiality which is his universality or divinity. So the meaning of expounding the spirituality as the religion of Man as the harmonious development of human nature in blending the religious, social, cultural values as his spirituality in leading to the expansion of humanity. Thus, this new idea of Man as the development of religious or spiritual potency with the development of humanity, finally establishes the socio-spiritual idea of Man as the development of the philosophy of *Spiritual Humanism*.

In this context, we may evaluate Vivekananda's Philosophy of Man as the conceptual identity as absolute oneness of man as done by academic philosophers but Swamiji develops a new synthetic method of evaluating the humanistic idea and its experience, spiritualistic awareness along with its socio-cultural impact on the expansion of the spirit of universality, culminating the intercultural prospect.

In the Introductory Note of present work, I have explained the fundamental objectives and principles of the treatise and in other seven parts under four chapters, I have made a critical and comparative study of the different problems and prospects of man in the light of the vision of Swami Vivekananda. I have tried to discuss all these chapters with much humility and caution. But in spite of this I am not sure if I have been able to avoid errors which are but inevitable in such a subject, critical and technical one. I shall always welcome any constructive criticism or suggestion in this regard.

The volume is prepared in conformity with the ideas and ideals of the International Society for Intercultural Studies and Research which is designed to promote exchange and intercommunication of attitudes and outlooks of different thinkers on an international platform with a view to providing scope for cultivating universality in quest of peace. In this background, I may submit that this work has been completed under the direction and guidance of the learned members of the society.

To make this programme more effective and comprehensive, our society-ISISAR has selected two distinguished scholars from India and USA to write foreward for exchanging their views on reflections upon the present theme from East-West perspectives. In this context I express my thankfulness to the members of ISISAR and gratefully acknowledge the contributions of Professor Amiya Kumar Majumdar, Former UGC Professor of Philosophy and well known scholar and activist on Sri Ramakrishna-Vivekananda movement and Dr Yeager Hudson, Professor of Philosophy, Colby College, University of Maine, Waterville, USA, a reputed Ideologist, in developing the theme from Intercultural perspective.

I am indebted to Dr Anil Kumar Sarkar of California State University, USA and Dr Kalidas Bhattacharya of Visvabharati, Santiniketan and Dr T.M.P. Mahadevan of Madras University, Chennai, India, who have directed and guided me to develop the present theme from contemporary thoughts from India and the West. My indebtedness to Swami Lokeswarananda, Secretary, The Sri Ramakrishna Mission Institute of Culture, Golpark, Kolkata, India who inspired me to enter into the theme by inviting me to deliver 'Kasi Saudamini Memorial Lectures' on 'The Religion of Man and Swami Vivekananda' in 1987. I also got much inspiration from Professor Sankari Prasad Basu, a noted Vivekananda scholar, Dr Sudhir Kumar Nandi, an eminent scholar on Aesthetics for their constant direction. I am really unfortunate that they are no more in this world when this book is brought to light.

I am thankful to Professor Gobinda Chandra Bandopadhyay, Professor Maniklal Bandopadhyay, Professor Chhanda Chatterjee, Dr Sudipto Chatterjee, Smt. Somdutta Chatterjee, Master Somdipto and Sri Ram Krishna Mondal for their co-operation in direct and in direct ways.

I am again Thankful to my publisher Gyan Publishing House, New Delhi for bringing out this volume.

I shall be rewarded if this work can stimulate the readers.

Dr Santi Nath Chattopadhyay

'Uttoran'–22, S.K. Deb Road
(4th bye lane), Kolkata–700 048
Phone: 091 33 2521 5753/2534 3782
E-mail: cal.isisar@gmail.com
Web: www. isisar.weebly.com

'Foreword' from East-West Perspectives

I

Western Perspective

Santi Nath Chattopadhyay's work–MAN, The Spiritual, continues the creative approach begun in R.N. Tagore's Philosophy of Man, an approach which combines the study of a major figure in recent Indian thought with the examination of wider humanistic and religious themes in Indian Philosophy. It will make a valuable contribution to contemporary philosophical discussion of the spirituality of humanistic religious thought such as that of Tagore, Vivekananda and others.

I

I see my role in the analysis of the Western view on this work, as bringing the perspective of Western philosopher to bear upon the work of Vivekananda and to a certain extent, the work of Chattopadhyay. What I would like to do is to say a few things about Vivekanada's career in the West, what he did and how Westerners responded to him, and to develop and comment on a short list of the most important ideas found way from his thought into American philosophical and religious thinking.

His persuasive advocacy of an attitude of open-mindness and tolerance among the religions of the world was a message to many Westerners greatly needed to hear. The religious traditions of India were not widely known in the United States in the late nineteenth century even among university professors of religious studies and much less among ordinary citizens. Serious misconceptions were widespread contributing to a condescending attitude which regarded Hinduism, at best as backward and unenlightened, and at worst as barbarous.

Vivekananda's hearers were astonished at the brilliance and charm of this learned Swami, and the richness and sophistication of religious tradition which he succeeded in communicating in such an attractive and persuasive way. The open-minded and tolerant attitude he conveyed stood in stark contrast to the intolerant attitude of superiority- if not of exclusiveness- so characteristic of Western religious thought, especially Christianity. And his great skill in the use of analogies, metaphors and stories to convey his teachings made it possible for him to capture the interest of a wide audience of both professional religious teachers and of lay persons. The eventual establishment of Vedanta Societies in a number of American cities contributed substantially to the growth of knowledge and understanding of Indian religion in the United States, and helped to keep alive the interest that Vivekananda had excited. Many of these societies are still active, a hundred years later.[1] A publication concern has been added which not only makes available the works of Vivekananda, and his master, Sri Ramakrishna, but also publishes material written by contemporary scholars and Swamis in the *Vedanta* tradition.

II

It can be said without fear of contradiction that the single most important idea propagated by Vivekananda during the two periods of time that he travelled and lectured in the United States is the idea that all religions are expressions of a common human longing for the divine, and as such contain essential truth. It was, a message that the West greatly needed but was not eager to hear. The second half of the nineteenth century was a time when many Christian denominations were engaged in intensive missionary activity designed to convert the peoples of the world to Christianity. It was not uncommon to hear missionary advocates appealing to the central governing bodies of their denominations in the United States for expanded funding, declaring that with proper effort, the whole world could be converted to Christianity within a century. India was the target of much such activity.

Calcutta was a centre of vigorous missionary work and Vivekananda had encountered there the attitudes of superiority and condescension so characteristic of the preachers. He was well acquainted, of course, with the efforts of Ram Mohun Roy to communicate to the Baptist Missionaries of Calcutta a sense of the high spiritual quality of Hinduism, and to persuade them to take a sense of the high spiritual quality of Hinduism, and to persuade them to take somewhat more open-minded attitude toward the religion and culture of their host country. But the missionary effort was postulated on the assumption that the Christian religion was the only true one, and that indeed all persons who were not Christians were condemned. It was urgent, therefore, that every human being be reached and persuaded to accept the message of Christ. To the missionaries, there was no question of mutual understanding or sharing of religious ideas.

Fortunately this attitude, so characteristic of several Christian denominations, was not universal in the United States. A few intellectuals had begun to study the Hindu scriptures in the early nineteenth century, and a measure of open-mindedness existed among several of the more liberal religious denominations. There remained a residue of the intellectual hospitality of the Enlightenment thought and religious rationalism characteristic of the late 1700's. The transcendentalist thinkers, Ralph Waldo Emerson and Henry David Thoreau, read such translations of the Indian classical writings as they could obtain, particularly translated portions of the *Upanishads* and the *Bhagavad Gita*. The idea of the oneness of God and Man, a core teaching of *Advaita Vedanta*, resonated both with Emerson's *Unitarianism* and with his own personal religious insights. In his celebrated essay titled *Nature* he writes of experiences when the veil separating the individual soul and the Divine Being is pulled away and we apprehend, if even for a brief moment, that we are "part and particle of God."[2] His essay titled *The Oversoul* also develops the notion of the inseparable oneness of the human soul with the *Oversoul*, which is the great Soul of the Universe.[3] And his poem, *Brahma*, reflects explicit influences from the Indian scriptures and expresses the core teaching that *Atman*, the human soul, is *Brahman*, the absolute reality.[4] Through his work as a popular lecturer and essayist Emerson spread these ideas to a wide audience in the United States, preparing the ground in some measure for the seed soon to be sown by

Vivekananda. The American intelligentsia, had met with Indian religious and philosophical ideas in the work of Thoreau and Walt Whitman.

Still, when Vivekananda arrived in the United States in 1893 to attend the Parliament of Religions, he found the American public neither well-informed nor very open-minded about *Hinduism*. Many Americans who did not dismiss it as benighted paganism treated it simply as a curiosity. The newspaper articles that reported on Vivekananda's lectures often reflected a substantial, sometimes startling, naivete.[5] Vivekananda patiently explained that widow-burning was no more typical in modem India than witch-burning was in modern America, and that the use of idols in Hindu worship was not really different in principle from the Roman Catholic use of statues or other symbols such as the cross.

His teaching that God is revealed in all of the world's religions and that no one religion has a monopoly on truth was thus a greatly needed corrective to the widespread belief that only Christianity reveals religious truths. It is an insight which still has not seeped adequately into the consciousness of religious Americans, but the graphic way in which Vivekananda put it made the point something that otherwise closed-minded Christians could at least consider. He cited the Bengali who spoke of *Jal, the Marathi* who spoke of *Pani,* and the Englishman who spoke of water, all using different terms to name the same thing. And he spoke of several paths at the foot of the mountain, leading off apparently in opposite directions, but all converging eventually at the mountain top. It is interesting to note that today, a hundred years later, such American advocates of religious tolerance and understanding as John Hick and John Cobb are still making, use of Vivekananda's approach of devising stories, analogies and metaphors to make precisely the same point about multiple mediators of the same message.[6]

To thoughtful philosophical and religious thinkers in all parts of the world it is becoming increasingly obvious that mutual religious misunderstanding with its concomitant suspicion, hostility and even overt fighting is one of the world's most dangerous problems. The great Catholic theologian, Hans Kung, makes the point thus: "There will be no peace among the peoples of this world without peace among the world religions."[7] No longer are the separate communities and nations bastions of a singlc religion. Virtually every major religion is present in nearly every country, Hindus and Christians, Muslims and Buddhists, Jews and Sikhs and Jains are rubbing elbows in nearly every corner of the world. It is therefore urgent that the attitude of tolerance and mutual understanding which was the central theme of Vivekananda's, and his master, Sri Ramakrishna's gospel be assimilated in every community. The only way that religious warfare can be ended is by the cultivation of mutual understanding and respect. This means that while the divergent teachings of the various religions must all be respected and tolerated, what can not be tolerated is an attitude of intolerance which asserts exclusivist claims.

It is becoming increasingly evident that Vivekananda's approach to the relations of the various religions to one another is the one that most needs to be heard in the world today. To dissolve one's own religion into some new religion is, at best unappealing and at worse, intensely threatening to most religious persons. But Vivekananda made it clear that this was not what he was advocating. Neither did he favour converting all people to a single existing religion nor making all the inhabitants of particular region devotees of the same religion. What he advocated was a sharing and mutual understanding which would help each individual to appreciate and practice his or her own religion more faithfully. "Do I wish that the Christian would become Hindu? God forbid. Do I wish that the Hindu or Buddhist would become Christian? God forbid.... But each must assimilate the spirit of the others and yet preserve his individuality and grow according to his own law of growth. The world has been very slow to recognise the absolute urgency of Vivekananda's message about mutual religious respect and understanding. But such success as is being achieved is along the lines Vivekananda advocated. There is perhaps no single message that the world needs more urgently to hear and to assimilate than this core teaching of the great Swami.

III

The specific content of Vivekananda's philosophical teachings,- his interpretation on the non-dualism of *Advaita Vedanta*, fell on less fertile ground in the West and especially in the United States. To be sure, there was the tradition of philosophical monism in the form of absolute idealism taught in England by such thinkers as F. H. Bradley and in the United States by Josiah Royce, but this was always a minority position and was being increasingly crowded out during the nineteenth century by several rising movements in Western philosophy. There are interesting affinities between Vivekananda's Vedanta philosophy and absolute idealism as advocated by Westerners, but there are important dissimilarities as well. And it was not the absolute idealists who made contact with Vivekananda and attempted to follow and respond to his work.

The most influential philosophical movement in the United States during the time that Vivekananda was lecturing in the West was *Pragmatism*. Indeed, it remains the predominant American philosophy today. The Pragmatists were not very much interested in metaphysics-although they were not explicitly hostile to it as the logical positivists were and their discussions with the absolute idealists such as Bradley and Royce gave them a distinct distaste for monistic views. John Dewey, a leading Pragmatist, explicitly denounced dualism but to the extent that he developed a non-dualist metaphysics, it was a version of evolutionary naturalism which much more closely resembled the position of S. Radhakrishnan than that of Vivekananda.

Among the Pragmatists, it was William James who made the most explicit effort to connect his views with Vivekananda's *Vedanta* teachings. James was the only one of the leading Pragmatists who had a substantial interest in religion. He produced a ground-breaking work on the psychology and philosophy of religious experience and mysticism which included a study of most of the major religious and mystical traditions of the world. Vivekananda seems to have been his major source, for information about *Hinduism*. He quotes extensively from the lectures and writings of the Swami and is particularly interested in Vivekananda's interpretation of *Raja Yoga*. Despite his rationalist/empiricist approach, James is very careful to insist that the critical philosopher must pay close and fair attention to the reported experiences of mystics. Indeed, it is in the name of *empiricism* that James insists that religious experience should he regarded as a source of the raw material for knowledge along with sense experience.

That people have religious experiences that these experiences-are as real as any other kinds of experiences is something that no scientist or philosopher can legitimately doubt.

One conclusion that most mystics and some philosophers have reached on the basis of mystic experience is that all reality is one. This is as true of Western absolute idealism as it is of Eastern. *Advaita Vedanta*, although, of course, the details of the interpretations of ultimate reality differ. James recognises that the almost irresistible force of mystical experience, whether Western or Eastern, whether Christian, Buddhist, or Hindu is the firm conviction that in that experience the individual actually apprehends directly, in an unmediated way, not only the complete oneness of all reality, but more important, his or her own oneness with the ultimate One.

He points out that we sometimes have sense experiences which give us the overwhelming sense that some object is before us or that some phenomenon has been apprehended, but reflection on these experiences leads us to reinterpret them. To make them coherent with a more comprehensive view of reality it is sometimes necessary to reject the surface appearance of even a very vivid sense experience. Likewise with mystical experiences, such a reinterpretation may be necessary. James even suggests that the unshakable conviction about the complete oneness of ultimate reality which characterises such absolute idealists as his Harvard University colleague, Josiah Royce, may derive as much from mystical as from-rational considerations. It is undoubtedly true, James agrees, that some persons sometimes experience reality as one and themselves inseparably identified with the ultimate. It is also true, he argues, that all of us experience plurality most of the time and this experience also carries considerable weight. James admits that in the final accounting the experienced oneness of the mystics and the non-dualist philosophical teachings of the idealists and the Advaitists may turn out to be the truth. But he finds the evidence for plurality so extensive and pervasive, all out of proportion with that for oneness, that he concludes that we cannot, as empiricist philosophers, justify dismissing it in favour of monism at this stage in our process of seeking understanding.

So James affirms himself a pluralist *for the time being,* while expressing his readiness to revise his view and convert to monism if the evidence sufficiently accumulates in that direction.[10] Even so, his respect for *Advaita Vedanta* and particularly for the work of Vivekananda is unmistakable. James' references to Vivekananda, and the extensive quotations from his lectures and writings in James' own works, did a great deal, to bring the Swami's thought to the attention of many American philosophers who otherwise might not have noticed it. And James was in complete agreement with Vivekananda's sentiments about open-mindedness in attitude and methodology as we seek philosophical understanding, and about intellectual hospitality and mutual respect among the world's philosophical and religious traditions.

There is another point of strong affinity between James and Vivekananda. Both were eager to take the venerable message of philosophy out of the dusty libraries and the lofty ivory towers and make it available and appealing to ordinary people. James was convinced that philosophy is a tool for practical living, an instrument by means of which people may see and understand the significance of their lives and learn thus to live better lives. He was in complete agreement with his fellow-Pragmatist, John Dewey who insisted that philosophy ought to be a technique for dealing, not with the problems of philosophers, but with the problems of human persons.

Vivekananda also believed that the precious treasures of philosophy and the truths of the religious scriptures are intended for everyone, not just scholars and sannyasis. When he lectured in the West, he made it a point to connect his teachings with ideas with which he could be confident that his audience would already be familiar. He often juxtaposed illustrations from the Bible with those from the *Upanishads* or the *Bhagavad Gita*. In his teachings in India he recognised that even the most untutored villager is well acquainted with the stories of the great Indian classics such as the *Mahabharata and Ramayana,* and insisted that the doctrines of *Vedanta* can similarly he made understandable and memorable to ordinary people. In his lectures dealing with *Karma Yoga*, he emphasised how important it was that everyone understood the notion of working with non-attachment. All of the teachings of *Vedanta* are relevant to the lives of even the most lowly person, and can be made intelligible and meaningful to everyone, but *Karma Yoga* is especially appropriate as a popular path even for those in society who ordinarily believe that they are capable only of *Bhakti*.

IV

Some critics of Vivekananda imagined that they had detected an inconsistency between his strong support of the non-dualism of *Vedanta* doctrine on the one hand and his insistence that the calling of the *Vedanta* Math and Mission was as much to perform works of charity and social service as to pursue the life of contemplation. Does not *Advaita Vedanta*, especially as Sri Ramakrishna and Vivekananda interpret it, teach that *Atman is Brahman*, that the dualisms and dichotomies people imagine they see between humans and God, between human individuals and the universe, between a person and his or her brother or sister are is *maya*? In one of his lectures he calls upon the audience to imagine an individual looking from behind, a screen in which there is only a very small hole. The person would see only a tiny bit of what was beyond the screen. If we imagine the whole becoming bigger and bigger, the person comes to see more and more until the screen is taken away entirely and everything is visible. Surely we would not say that the person had to change, but only that he needed an enlarged vision. Similarly, it is not that we need, to strive to change so that we may become one with God or achieve perfection, but only to take away the veil that conceals from us the truth that we are already identical with God and thus that we are already perfect.

If this interpretation of the claim that *Atman is Brahman* is correct, say the critics, there is no place for a mission to help our suffering or benighted fellow human beings, because (1) they are already identical with God and certainly God could not be in need of anything; (2) they are already perfect and could not need any help; and (3) they and we are not separate beings, but are one with one another because there is actually only one reality; thus there is no suffering or benighted brother or sister to help. Furthermore, since the world is *maya,* illusion, we should not involve ourselves with it or imagine that we can improve it by acts of charity. Rather we should bend our efforts to overcome the illusion so that we plainly see that nothing needs to change-indeed, nothing ever could change because everything is already divine and perfect. To dedicate a lot of energy toward providing food, housing, clothing, and medical care for the bodies of other persons is to miss the true objective which is recognition of the ultimate unreality of the body and the falsity of our belief in suffering and need.

The problem of the relation of the ultimate One to the fluctuating multiple shadows of the material world has been a difficult one at least since the time of Plato in the West. The advocates of absolute idealism such as Hegel, Bradley and Royce, strove mightily to generate a theory to account for this relationship. Because monistic theories have been uncommon and have not benefited either from extensive exploration and elaboration nor extensive criticism and reworking in the West, they have not been worked out in as subtle and plausible ways as they have in India.

It is likely, too, that the predominance of Christian monotheistic theology with its dualistic metaphysics has made the West less ready to consider and less able to understand monistic positions. Indeed, most of the systems of absolute idealism generated in Europe and the United States have attempted not only to show how the material world can be both real and not real, but have also embraced at least in name the God of monotheistic Christianity. Hegel's approach to the problem of the One and the many was dialectic with the many, ultimately to be synthesised indeed with the many already synthesised, unrecognisedly so-in the Absolute. Hegel even includes the Christian doctrine of the trinity in his philosophy, recognising God the Son and God the Holy Spirit as dialectic phases in the culmination of reality in God the Father the Absolute One. Even so, Western thought never became comfortable with absolute idealism or with monism. And the question of charity and good works for fellow human beings, almost universally recognised among Westerners as a duty, has not been discussed in connection with any suggested unreality of the material world. Rather it has been connected with the Christian vision of the problem of evil, the problem, namely, of how evil and suffering could exist in a world created and controlled by an all-powerful and all-benevolent deity.

Vivekananda took both a theoretical and a practical approach to the problem raised by this criticism. By means of a notion of degrees or grades of reality, he interpreted the concept of *maya* to mean, not illusion or unreality, but incomplete understanding or less realised or less fulfilled reality. To be sure, ultimate reality is one, *Atman* is *Brahman*, humans are indeed perfect and divine but this does not mean that the illusion or dwarfed vision from which so many humans suffer is not in need of being addressed, and their suffering in need of alleviation. Vivekananda had very little patience with people who wanted to help the poor just by giving them religion. In an address at the Parliament of Religions he said, "You Christians, who are so fond of sending out missionaries to save the soul of the heathen-why do you not try to save their bodies from starvation? It is an insult to a starving people to offer them religion."[11]

No doubt, in the ultimate scheme of things, what is of greatest importance is *moksa*, but a poor, hungry, naked person can hardly even think about entering the path toward spiritual liberation until his bodily needs are in some measure satisfied. And so Vivekananda saw no inconsistency between the highest and most subtle doctrines of spirituality in *Advaita Vedanta* and the practice he prescribed for the members of his movement to feed the hungry, clothe the naked and bring material comfort to those in need. The wedding of thought and action and the effort by one's own hands to make human life more humane was of utmost importance. I suspect that this strong current of practicality and activism that William James recognised in the works of Vivekananda - a current which nicely matched James' own self-proclaimed belief that *Pragmatism* must be a philosophy of meliorism - accounts for the high respect of James had for Swamiji.

The mission to which Vivekananda felt called, and to which he called his brother disciples of Sri Ramakrishna, was two fold: spiritual and practical. This is why the movement he founded consists of two branches or functions, a Math and a Mission. The works of charity so essential among brothers and sisters who are in need must be firmly grounded in lives truly in touch with *Brahman*. Without doubt,

Raja Yoga is the royal path, but as Buddha refused *nirvana* until suffering brothers and sisters could be assisted along the way so also Vivekananda lifted up *Karma Yoga* as the path both to one's own liberation and to the aid, physical as well as spiritual, of fellow human beings. Without this practical and compassionate aspects of his work, Vivekananda might well have been what so many Indian holy men have been when they have tried to communicate a religious message in America. So many have come, preached, created a brief stir, and soon faded into oblivion. The influence of Vivekananda lives on in America because he spoke with meaning and inspiration to even the common person and because he saw the importance of making the treasures of philosophy and religion available to everyone, both through teaching and through compassionate service.

V

It is a hundred years since the great Swami brought his message of mutual respect and understanding to the West. Many other missions from the East have preached aspects of Indian philosophy in these intervening years. Most recently A.C. Bhaktivedanta Swami Prabhupada created a sizable stir, provoking considerable hostility but also winning a number of disciples and establishing missions all across the United States. Even after the death of the founder, the Hare Krishnas, as his disciples are called, continue to propagate the teaching through the Society for Krishna Consciousness. They operate temples, ashrams, schools for expatriate Indian children, and a publishing concern. They have attracted a number of wealthy disciples to the movement whose generous financial support assures continued activity. But the Society for Krishna Consciousness, despite its translations and interpretations of the Hindu scriptures and the scholarly books it distributes, is a narrow and dwarfed interpretation of *Hinduism*, indeed it is basically just a *bhakti* movement. It practices and preaches *Bhakti Yoga* almost exclusively. To its credit it has again awakened in the Western mind a consciousness of and a curiosity about *Hinduism*. Nevertheless, it is a thin impoverished vision of the Hindu tradition. When this movement is contrasted with the comprehensive richness of Vivekananda's *Vedantism*, which has an important place for all of the Hindu paths, and a strong emphasis on the higher and more noble, the importance of keeping Vivekananda's vision fresh in the consciousness of Indians and Westerns alike becomes altogether clear.

Vivekananda's vision of the religion of humanity is an enduring one; it speaks of the needs of our times as much as it did a hundred years ago; and there is in it the power to illuminate and to stir persons to action. It needs urgently to be presented again in a clear and attractive way, so that the attention of this generation of philosophers, religious studies teachers and ordinary people is attracted and captured. I am convinced that the work of Professor Chattopadhyay can contribute importantly to this worthy work. I recommend *Man, The Spiritual* enthusiastically, especially to my fellow Westerners who may not be conversant with *Vedanta*, because I believe it not only communicates the message of Vivekananda in an attractive contemporary form, but also because I believe that it will inspire its religious animosity and sectarianism represents one of the greatest threats to peace, Vivekananda's message of religious toleration, mutual respect and understanding is urgent.

Yeager Hudson
Professor of Philosophy,
Colby College,
Waterville.
Maine, USA.

Notes and References

1. At least seventeen societies function in the United States. There are also active societies in Argentina, Canada, England, France, the Netherlands, and Switzerland, among others.
2. Ralph Waldo Emerson, "Nature," in *The Complete works of Ralph Waldo Emerson,* Concord Edition (Boston and New York: Houghton, Mifflin and Company, 1904).
3. See "The Oversoul," in *Complete Works,* op. cit.
4. For a discussion of the Indian influence upon Emerson's work and the striking parallels between his thought and that of Rabindranath Tagore, see Yeager Hudson, *Emerson and Tagore: The Poet* as *Philosopher* (Notre Dame: Cross Roads Books, 1988).
5. One reporter evidently had never heard of Jainism. He misunderstood Vivekananda to be speaking of a religious group called giantism.

6. See, for example, John Hick, *God Has Many Names* (Philadelphia: Westminster Press, 1982), John B.Cobb, Jr., *Beyond Dialogue* (Philadelphia: Fortress Press, 1982), and Ninian Smart, *A Dialogue* of *Religions* (London: SCM Press), 1960.
7. Hans Kung et al., *Christianity and the World Religions* (Garden City, N.Y.: Doubleday, 1970).
8. "Address at the Final Session of the Parliament of Religions". *The Complete Works* of *Swami Vivekananda,* (Calcutta: Advaita Ashrama, 1989), Vol. 1, p. 24.
9. William James, *The Varieties of Religious Experience* (New York: Macmillan,1902).
10. See especially his *A Pluralistic Universe* (New York: Macmillan, 1909) and "The One and the Many," from *Pragmatism* (New York: Longmans, Green, 1907).
11. "Religion Not the Crying Need of India", *Complete Works,* Vol.1, p. 20.

II

Eastern Perspective

Dr Santi Nath Chattopadhyay has undertaken a commendable task of understanding Vivekananda from the eastern and western perspectives. It is his contention that so far as western philosophy is concerned, the doctrine of a philosopher can be studied apart from the life and experience of the philosopher concerned. In the case of eastern philosophy, however, to understand the philosophy of a thinker you have to first understand the man, for the eastern philosophers do not preach philosophy; they live it. In other words, the kind of philosophy a man has, depends on the kind of man he is. Dr Chattopadhyay affirms that in the philosophy of man as propounded by Vivekananda, "religion" is the key term. Religion harmonises both the internal and the external aspects of man. Spirituality, observes Dr Chattopadhyay, is not mere transcendentality. While on the one hand it is a process of transcendence of limitations or contradictions of life, on the other, it is an experiential process of realising value with its manifestations in human existence in different degrees.

Professor Hudson, as a representative of the Western countries, has attempted to give us an account of Vivekananda's career in the West, what he did and how westerners responded to him. I have been entrusted with the task of assessing the impact of Vivekananda's message from eastern perspective. Being fully aware of my limitations all that I propose to do is to say a few things on the subject somewhat baldly, keeping in view the comments of Professors Hudson and Chattopadhyay. I think, my duty will be to explore the meaning and nature of spirituality first and then to expand this idea in socio-cultural context, removing the prevalent misunderstandings in the matter.

I

The world of today is in the grip of severe tension - a tension which is due to a conflict of two opposing forces - one making for isolation, strife and divisiveness, the other making for global unity and global awareness. Man is in a dilemma because he fails to adjust his old beliefs, attitudes and loyalties to the new world in the context of the tremendous advance of science and technology. How can the tension be resolved? Vivekananda tells us that it is through the recognition of the spiritual oneness of mankind that the crisis can be averted.

What, precisely, is meant by spirituality? To be sure, spirituality is not clairvoyance, nor is it an art of transmitting information of the after-world through certain media. Spirituality has various shades of meanings and nuances. In the first place it emphasises the glory of man, man who is not a physico-chemical complex but spirit, soul or *Caitanya*. Truly speaking, man is potentially divine. Secondly, spirituality means pursuit of the science of the soul in order to manifest the divinity within. Thirdly, an individual's happiness lies in the happiness of the community. Spiritual life is a life where the ego-centred existence has been transformed into an 'all'- centred being. Fourthly, spirituality signifies that matter will ever remain a servant of spirit and not spirit of matter. Lastly, spirituality implies that the universe is to be looked upon as an integrated whole where man, nature and God are interrelated, as Vivekananda envisaged, modern science confirms this view.

It is important to bear in mind that spirituality is not opposed to materialism but to worldliness. Today, when man has been reduced to a commodity, a money-making machine, full of greed and possessive instincts, when man has forgotten his divine nature on account of his excessive dependence on matter, some adjustment on the spiritual plane is necessary.

Vivekananda observes: "From the orient came the voice which once told the world that if a man possesses everything that is under the Sun and does not possess spirituality, what avails it ? This is the ideal of the oriental type. For the occidental type, possession of material power is all that is to be coveted and that is all that is meant by progress and civilisation, and if there are other nations which do not care for possession of power, they are not fit to live."[1]

According to Vivekananda, "the oriental ideal is as necessary for the progress of the human race as the occidental, and I think it is more necessary."[2] He said: "The present adjustment will be the harmonising, the mingling of these, two ideals."[3] Instead of condemning materialism, Vivekananda recommends that some kind of harmony should be established between materialism and spirituality. Materialism must be there in so far as the physical well-being of man is concerned: yet *materialism* should not be regarded as an end in itself but as a means to an end. Whenever spirituality degenerates on account of the intervention and arrogance of priests who claim to be the sole custodians of spiritual wisdom, materialism serves as a corrective. What is needed for the progress of Indian society is that spirituality must be diffused throughout the length and breadth of the country and must not be allowed to remain concentrated in the lives of a few. Vivekananda says: "When the life blood is strong and pure no disease germ can live in that body. Our life blood is spirituality. If it flows clear, if it flows strong and pure, and vigorous, everything is right, political, social or any other material defects, *even the poverty the land* will all be cured if that blood is pure."[4]

Vivekananda makes a bold claim when he says that spirituality can cure even the poverty of the land. How is it possible? The common man believes that poverty arises when there is exploitation of the have-nots by the haves, when wealth is concentrated in the hands of a few. Vivekananda goes to the root of the matter and points out that it is the consciousness of spiritual unity that inspires people to release their boundless energy and undertake a concerted action so as to recreate conditions which will be conducive to the emergence of an egalitarian society. There have been numerous plans for removal of poverty. Unless, however, those who are entrusted with the task - and they are always a creative minority - as Arnold Toynbee has pointed out, act in a spirit of service and renunciation, the expected result might not be achieved. Here in lies the importance of the awareness of the spiritual solidarity of mankind.

Vivekananda urges that "the abstract Advaita must become living, poetic in everyday life:"[5] Yet, at the same time he tells us that the highest *Advaitism* cannot be brought down to practical life. Is there any inner contradiction between the two statements? If one studies Vivekananda deeply and critically, one will give a negative reply. According to Vivekananda, *Vedanta* preaches certain ideals, viz, that every being is potentially divine and consequently the difference between an amoeba and a human being is a difference in degree, not in kind. Secondly, to be theistic means to have faith in oneself and finally, every being of this universe is proceeding towards perfection and freedom.

It is true, indeed, that the ideal is, always, far ahead of the real or the practical. When one talks of actualisation of the ideal, one has to keep in mind certain basic facts. There are two tendencies in human nature: one, to harmonise the ideal with the existing life, and the other, to elevate this life to the ideal. It is important to understand this, for the former tendency is the temptation of our lives. When a person recommends an ideal which requires me to give up selfishness, I hesitate to accept it, because, to my mind it is impractical. But when a person brings an ideal which can be reconciled with my selfishness I heartily accept it. This is the way the world moves.

It was pointed out by Vivekananda that our greatest mistake was to confine the teachings of the *Vedanta* to the spiritual life only; to the lives of the monks only. In fact, the teachings of the *Vedanta* were meant for people of all walks of life. Practical *Vedanta* signifies that the teachings of the *Vedanta*, viz, renunciation, service, truthfulness, self-control etc. are to be practised ceaselessly, until the aspirant's life is attuned to those ideals, that is to say, until the world becomes one with God.

One of the main teachings of the *Vedanta* is abolition of all privileges. Vivekananda speaks of four kinds of special privileges which constitute the bane of society. First, the claim of special privilege by the strong over the physically weak. Second, the claim of special privilege by the rich over the poor. Third, the claim of special privilege by the learned over the ignorant. Fourth, the claim of special privilege by a religious community which considers its religion to be the only truth and affirms that men of other faiths must embrace this religion in order to be redeemed. Since the *Vedanta* teaches oneness of being it can not, at the same time, accept special privileges for any particular group.

Professor Hudson has referred to Western critics' arguments that if the foundational truth is *Atman-Brahman*, then there is no scope for removal of suffering of the downtrodden and the exploited because they are already identical with *Brahman*, and already perfect and do not have any isolated existence. Besides, since the world is *maya* or illusion there is no point in saying that we can improve the nature of the world by acts of charity. But Vivekananda has clearly explained why and how this can be done.

II

According to Vivekananda, *maya* does not mean illusion. "The Maya of the Vedanta" he says "in its last developed form, is neither Idealism nor Realism, nor is it a theory. It is a simple statement of facts what we are and what we see around us."[6] Let us enumerate some of the facts stated by Vivekananda. It is common experience that man's powers are limited: he realises his helplessness before the vast forces of nature; he fails to comprehend the infinite truth, infinite, intelligence and infinite love. This limitation of power or capacity is a fact which nobody can deny. Again, we know that death is the inevitable end of everything. The great cities and empires built by men with care and skill, all our progresses and achievements, our vanities and reforms, have that one end-destruction i.e., death. And yet people cling to life. We do not know why we cling to life, when we know that death is the end. Again, it is our experience that very often we cannot do good to others, except through evil. Animals are living upon plants, men upon animals, and worst of all, upon one another the strong upon the weak. This is going on everywhere and this is *maya.* We are often told that, in the long run, everything will be good. But why should good come out of evil? Why cannot good be done through good alone? There is no solution of this problem, and this is *maya.* As we increase our power to be happy, we also increase our power to suffer. The more we have material progress, the more are opened the avenues to both pleasure and pain. This, again, is *maya.* The same thing which is the source of unhappiness and misery in one case, may produce happiness in another. The fire that burns a child may cook a good meal for a starving man. This is *maya.*

The upshot of the entire discussion is apparently this: *Maya* is neither *sat* nor *asat,* neither real nor unreal. Only the ultimate reality or Brahman is *sat.* And from this point of view, *maya* is certainly *asat* or unreal. Nevertheless it is not zero or nothing, for had it been so sense objects could not have been created by *meya.* The non-dual *Vedanta* affirms that *Brahman* is both the *material and the efficient cause of the universe. Advaitism* (non-dualistic *Vedanta*), is, according to Vivekananda, "the fairest flower of philosophy and religion that any country in any age has produced, where human thought attains its highest expression and even goes beyond the mystery which seems to be impenetrable. It is too abstruse, too elevated, to be the religion of the masses. Even in India, its birth place, where it has been ruling supreme for the three thousand years, it has not been able to permeate the mases."[7] That is the reason why Vivekananda was anxious to make *Advaita Vedanta* practical in everyday life, to spread the message of the *Advaita* everywhere, in the temple of worship, in the court of law, in the eating house, in the study of a student.

Since *Brahman* is all-pervading it is certainly present in the poor, the downtrodden, the exploited, but it is present in a dormant state. On account of ignorance and as a result of century-long tyranny by the upper class, the downtrodden people have forgotten that they also are divinities on earth. Vivekananda says, "our aristocratic ancestors went on treading the common masses of our country under foot till they became helpless, till under this torment the poor people nearly forgot that they were human beings. They have been compelled to be merely hewers of wood and drawers of water for centuries, so much so that they are made to believe that they are born as slaves."[8]

So the uplift of the masses was the primary concern of Vivekananda. His maxim was: "First bread, then religion." What, then, is the plan of action recommended by Vivekananda for removal of poverty?

To acquaint the people with the main tenets of *Vedantic Socialism* and urge them to work in a spirit of selfless service so as to ameliorate the pitiable condition of the messes. His advice is: break not, pull not anything down, but build. He respected the standpoint of each worker and came forward to help him grow according to the nature of his being. Although there are thousands and thousands of varieties of mind and inclinations, yet, for practical purposes, human nature has been classified into four types, the worker, the devotee, the philosopher and the mystic. The first type loves to work and through work, performed selflessly, wants to reach freedom. The second, the devotee, does not care whether God's existence can be proved or not, but loves the sublime and the beautiful. He loves, with all his heart, the great souls of all times. The philosopher is keen on knowing the nature of reality through his intellectual faculty. He wants to weigh everything on the scale of reason, before reaching any conclusion. The mystic tries to analyse his own mind and see what forces are there to guide him and how he can control those inward forces in order to know the truth.

According to Vivekananda, the goal of human life is to manifest the divinity within, by controlling nature, external or internal. Freedom can be achieved by manifesting the inward divinity by work or worship, by psychic control or philosophy. One may undertake any method suitable to one's temperament or all the four.

It is widely known that Vivekananda declared that he was a socialist, but at the same time he warned that *Socialism* was not a perfect system but "half a loaf is better than no bread". He felt that *Socialism* was well worth trying. He urged, however, that *Socialism* must be based on *Advaita Vedanta*.

What Vivekananda meant by the *Vedantic* foundation of *Socialism* is expressed in his long essay entitled "Modern India". Says he "The individual's life is in the life of the whole, the individual's happiness is in the happiness of the whole, apart from the whole, the individual's existence is inconceivable - this is an eternal truth and is the bed-rock on which the universe is built. To move slowly towards the infinite whole, bearing a constant feeling of intense sympathy and sameness with it, being happy with the happiness and being distressed in its affliction, is the individual's sole duty."[8a]

Vivekananda was fully appreciative of the role of material civilisation. Said he: "We speak foolishly against material civilisation... in all India there are, say; a hundred thousand really spiritual men and women. Now, for the spiritualisation of these, must the three hundred million be sunk in savagery and starvation? Why should anyone starve?...Material civilisation, nay, even luxury is necessary to create work for the poor. Bread, Bread! I do not believe in a God who cannot give me bread here, giving me eternal bliss in heaven."[8b]

He appreciated the role of materialism in society but did not minimise the importance of spirituality. Vivekananda, who had a keen sense of history, tells us that two attempts have been made to found social life in the world. One is founded on spirituality, the other on materialism. It appears from a study of social evolution that at times the spiritual side prevails and thereafter the materialistic side. They follow each other in wave-like motions. Materialistic ideas prevail for some time, gradually grow and encompass the entire society and attaining prosperity, start degenerating. Then spirituality comes to the rescue of society curbing competition and cruelty as also jealousy and hatred. Spirituality produces a class of people who lay exclusive claim on the special power of the world and a time comes when "not only all the spiritual power of the race, but all its material powers and privileges are centred in the hands of a very few; and these few standing on the necks of the masses of the people want to rule them. Then society has to help itself, and materialism comes to the rescue."[9] Yet, at the same time, Vivekananda warns that excessive materialism will also mean disaster. "The material tyranny is tremendous. The wealth and power of a country are in the hands of a few men who do not work but manipulate the work of millions of human beings. By this power they can deluge the whole earth with blood...The western world is governed by a handful of Shylocks. All those things that you hear about–constitutional government, freedom, liberty, and parliaments are but jokes. The West is groaning under the tyranny of the priests; each must keep the other in check."[10]

Two chief conclusions emerge from the foregoing observations of Vivekananda: (1) The excess of materialism degenerating into consumerism is to be curbed by spirituality: (2) The excess of spirituality degenerating into perversion is to be curbed by materialism. Besides, one has to keep it in mind that the material progress and prosperity of our country are due to the silent work done by the labouring classes of India who have given their heart's blood and, in return, have been trampled by the upper class.

In passing, I may refer to Dr Chattopadhyay's observations. According to him, the idea of divinity of man is a synthesis of materiality and spirituality in the development of human existence, expanding the creative philosophy of man as the philosophy of spiritual man. To my mind, it seems that in Vivekananda's view, materialism and spirituality are complementary half-truths. When materialism goes astray, spiritualism acts as a corrective. Similarly, when spiritualism goes astray, materialism acts as a corrective. To say that man is potentially divine is to affirm that he has infinite possibilities and that his essential nature is freedom. On account of ignorance he is oblivious of his essential nature, yet he has an Intense longing for realising it.

III

I am afraid I cannot fully share the view of Professor Hudson when he says that when Vivekananda arrived at the United States in 1893 to attend the Parliament of Religions, he found the American public neither well-informed nor very open-minded about *Hinduism*.

In has already been stated that Vivekananda considered the lofty teachings of *Advaita Vedanta* somewhat abstract and difficult to be grasped by the common people. The question naturally arises as to whether the intellectual climate of America was congenial and receptive enough to assimilate the refreshingly original and almost revolutionary ideas presented by Vivekananda before the '*Parliament of Religions*' (1893). It is true, indeed, that during the last decade of the nineteenth century America was a materialistic wasteland where industrialisation was slowly but surely advancing in a measurable degree. One cannot, however afford to forget that there were other forces at work also during the period of Vivekananda's visit to America. The comparative study of religion introduced by Ram Mohun Roy had made a deep impression on the idealistic movement sponsored by the members of the Transcendentalist Club. Ten Great *Religions* by James Freeman Clarke, published in 1871 was a notable contribution to comparative religion. In his introduction to *The Age of Fable* (1881), Reverend Edward Hale wrote: "During the last fifty years new attention has been paid to the system of religion of the Eastern world. Even young caders will take an interest in such books as Clarke's Great Religions and Johnson's Oriental Religions."[11]

It appears from these facts that both serious and casual leaders had access to a considerable portion of materials concerning Indian religions. Max Mueller and Ralph Waldo Emerson were great friends. As a token of love and gratitude Mueller sent Emerson a copy of the former's *Introduction to the Science of Religion.* That was in 1873. Max Mueller's greatest achievement in spreading knowledge about Indian religions in the West was his editorship of *The Sacred Books of the East* (1875-1900). There are still other factors which go to prove that the intellectual climate of America, when Vivekananda visited the country, was favourable for dissemination of the Swami's ideas and ideals. Even during his stay in America when the Parliament was in session, Vivekananda inspired William James, an avowed pluralist, a philosopher and psychologist of great eminence. Although Romain Rolland does not admit that in systematising his philosophical and religious views William James was inspired by Vivekananda.[12]

Yet a careful reader will not fail to notice that the observations made by William James in his *Varieties of Religious Experience* clearly show that despite his being a pluralist he did not fail to catch a glimpse of the 'monistic music' which Vivekananda presented. William James says: "If religion be a function by which either God's, cause or man's cause is to be really advanced, then he who lives the life of it, however narrowly is a better servant than he who merely knows about it, however much. Knowledge about life is one thing, effective occupation of a place in life, with its dynamic currents passing through your being is another".[13]

Although Vivekananda was a monist (a non-dualist, to be precise) and William James a pluralist, yet both regarded philosophy as a tool to be used for the betterment of society. That William James' reverence for Vivekananda was deep and unbounded, will be evident from the profuse quotations from Vivekananda's writings in his works.

It is important to bear in mind that the Indian attitude to reality is subjective, inward and mystical. The inner unity is *Atman* and the outer unity is *Brahman.* But they are not separate, they are identical. That is why the motto of the highest code of ethics is "Not me but thou". The "me" is the manifestation of the infinite and so also is "Thou". The most important aspect of the teachings of the *Vedanta* is this: By thinking intensely of the good of others, by devoting yourself to the service, you will purify your heart by that work and through it you will have the vision of the Supreme Self which permeates all living and non-living beings. Having realised the transcendental stage the saint sees the Self (*Atman*) in all beings and all beings in the Self and possessed of this knowledge he devotes himself to the service of others. Theoretical knowledge, however, is not enough. One has to practice, find means for attaining Truth. As Sri Ramakrishna used to say: "You cannot get butter by crying yourself hoarse, saying there is butter in the milk. If you wish to make butter, you must turn the milk into curd, and churn it well...So If you long to see God, practice spiritual disciplines. What is the use of merely crying, "Lord! Lord!"."

Realisation of Self does not make a person indifferent to the world, does not prompt his to remain in isolation. Rather spiritual realisation inspires him to lay down his life for the good of others. Swami Saradarianda, in his *Sri Ramakrishna Lila Prasanga* tells us that Sri Ramakrishna remained immersed in *nirvikalpa samadhi,* in the bliss of union with Brahman, for six months. He did not have any normal consciousness during the period. But at last he received the Mother's command: "Remain in *Bhavamukha* for the good of mankind."[14] The important point is to be noted is 'for the good of mankind' not for one's own salvation. *Bhavamukha* is a state between *samadhi* and normal consciousness.

The Indian attitude, in so far as spiritual experience is concerned, has been summed up by Vivekananda thus: "Do not depend on doctrines, or sects, or churches, or temples; they count for little compared with the essence of existence in man, which is divine; and the more this divinity is developed in man, the more powerful is he for good. Earn that spirituality first, acquire that, and criticise no one, for all doctrines and creeds have some good in them. Show by your lives that religion does not mean words, or names, or sects, but that it means spiritual realisation. Only those can understand who have perceived the Reality. Only those who have attained spirituality can communicate it to others, can be great leaders of making. They alone are the power of light."[15]

The conclusions which emerge from the foregoing discussion may be set forth thus: (a) Spiritual enlightenment and social activity are not mutually antagonistic; rather, a social worker becomes a better worker when he derives sustenance from spiritual experience and arms himself with spiritual power; (b) all religions are equally valid and no one religion has a monopoly of truth; (c) religious fanaticism and bitterness between one religion and another can be cured by cultivation of mutual understanding and respect; (d) awareness of the spiritual solidarity of mankind as a whole goes a long way in establishing peace and harmony in the world; (e) to serve man as an embodiment of God is the highest ideal before mankind.

In the light of these observations, I may evaluate the total programme on Man. The Spiritual and the viewpoint of Dr Chattopadhyay when he emphasises, "...The development of creative Unity in multi-dimensional forms as diversities, with the expression of Universality in peace, which; in the observation of Vivekananda, is the expansion of the divine world order." In this context, Arnold Toynbee's warning is worth quoting. In his Foreword to Swami Ghanananda's book *Sri Ramakrishna and His Unique Message* (1970), Toynbee said: "In the present age, the world has been united on the material plane by Western technology. But this Western skill has not only "annihilated distance", it has armed the peoples of the world with weapons of devastating power at a time when they have been brought to point-blank range of each other without yet having learnt to know and love each other. At this supremely dangerous moment in human history, the only way of salvation for mankind is an Indian way. The Emperor Ashoka's and Mahatma Gandhi's principle of non-violence and Sri Ramakrishna's testimony to the harmony of religions; here we have the attitude and the spirit that can make it possible for the human race to grow together into a single family and in the Atomic Age his is the only alternative to destroying ourselves."

Amiya Kumar Mazumdar

Former UGC Professor of Philosophy, Associated with different Administrative Services and closely associated with Sri Ramakrishna–Vivekananda Movement and former president of ISISAR (Internatinal Society for Intercultural Studies and Research), Kolkata, India.

References

1. Complete Works, 1963, Vol. IV, p. 155.
2. *Ibid.*
3. *Ibid.*
4. C W 1963, Vol. III, p. 288.
5. C W 1963, Vol. V, p. 104.
6. C W 1963, Vol. II, p. 89.
7. C W 1963, Vol. II, p. 247.
8. C W1963, vol. III, p. 192.

8a. C W 1963, Vol. IV, p. 463.

8b. C W 1963, Vol. IV, p. 368.

9. C W 1963, Vol. III, p. 157.
10. C W 1963, Vol. III, p. 159.
11. *Swami Vivekananda and America* by Professor Amiya Kumar Mazumdar and Fred Trembour, USIS, 1963, p. 11.
12. *The Life of Vivekananda and Universal Gospel* by Romain Rolland, 1992, p. 87.
13. *The Varieties* of *Religious Experience* by William James, 1963, p. 497.
14. *Sri Ramakrishna Lilaprasanga,* Part I, pp. 61-2.
15. C W 1963, Vol. IV, pp. 182-3.

Introductory Note

The present work aims at discussing the problems of the philosophy of man in the background of the humanistic analysis of religion as the fundamental basis of the Indian tradition and culture. In this context the terms philosophy of religion and culture, in a humanistic sense are closely associated with one another to the examination of the natural existence of man as his harmonious development of life with the proper realisation of human values.

For the evaluation of this humanistic programme, the present work centres round the idea of the Spiritual Man, as examined by Swami Vivekananda as an explanation of human existence in a very natural way. Thus, in analysing the philosophy of man, Vivekananda uses the term religion for the natural analysis of internal and external aspects of man in a synthetic form. The internal aspects, of man refer to the intellectual and emotional or mental are closely associated with each other for the synthetic evaluation of mental and social or individual and collective existence of human life.

For this Gisbert evaluates the meaning of religion in a synthetic form and thus observes, "the role religion in life manifests itself in the individual by giving him an integrated outlook on life...."[1]

Religion in this integrated sense of explaining the human nature, fulfills the cultural significance of life which is to be understood as the satisfaction of material and non-material or aesthetic and spiritual interests of life. The material objects with the patterns or the ways in which these are produced, express the material culture of man. With this material process, man also reveals his non-material interest, expressing his creative potency of mind through the aesthetic and spiritual activities which are to be recognised as mental culture.

Both these forms of culture are closely related to the humanistic idea of religion, revealing the internal and external aspects of man.

So, religion, in this humanistic sense, stands for culture, explaining the material and mental existence of man in a natural form which is the examination of the human existence as the natural expression of life. Thus, in the explanation of the cultural importance of religion as manifestation of human nature, Gisbert again explains, "...Culture is the direct expression of our nature; in our ways of thought and action, in art, religion, morality and recreation. It deals with interests and values conceived as ends, to which various actions and objects are directed as means."[2] So this religio-cultural significance of human life means 'the direct expression of our nature' which deals with the ideas or values and expressions or activities, explaining the philosophy of man.

For this natural explanation of the philosophy of man as the religio-cultural significance of life, a novel programme of the religion of man is introduced for examining religion as the natural or cultural expression of human existence. In this natural process of expressing the religion of life, it is found that religion is not to be taken as the imposition of value on man as suggested by different religions in traditional or ordinary sense, but value in the background of the idea of the religion of man, is to be treated as the natural expression of the creative potency in human existence as *Manava Dharma* (human nature).

In the analysis of the creative potency, Vivekananda uses the term 'perfection' which is expressed through different values explained as humanistic in nature. This process explains the true nature of the religion of man which is neither supernaturalism as the imposition of dogmas on man, nor is the performance of mere religious rites and ceremonies. It, on the other hand, is the natural expression and realisation of human values, potential in man. This may be explained in the words of Mackenzie as, " ...the spirit that inspires the best forms of constructive or creative work may be described as religious."[3] This type of religious process is a humanistic programme of developing human personality through the 'constructive or creative' activities for the realisation of human values. So, religion, in this humanistic sense, is recognised as the religion of man which, according to Vivekananda, makes religion intimate to human existence, explaining the natural expression of man as the realisation of human values. Thus, religion of man as the realisation of human values becomes the religion of humanity as a synthesis of values. This, according to Vivekananda, is a process of becoming which he evaluates not as a supernatural or unnatural process but as a natural humanistic process of developing potential infiniteness or universality through the expression of human values in different creative states of existence.

Creative expression of values, developing creative state of universality, consists in the recognition of the highest value of unity in life which, in the observation of Vivekananda, is divine or spiritual in a transcendent-experiential form. The realisation of this highest value of unity in human existence is to be recognised as the embodiment of transcendent unity as godness or universality through the experiential forms of realising human values of truth, beauty and goodness, manifesting perfection as godness or universality in different creative states of existence as developing unity or harmony in life and existence.

So, the spirituality, in the observation of Vivekananda, is not mere transcendentality. It, on the other hand, stands for the transcendent value, manifested and realised in different creative states of existence in different degrees. So, this creative process on one hand is a process of transcendence of limitations or contradictions of life and on the other hand, it also is an experiential process of realising value with its manifestations in human existence in different degrees, reconciling contradictions in unity.

Thus, spiritual process, according to Vivekananda, may be treated as a creative process of synthesis that stands for value with expression which explains the synthetic development of human existence. In this process, Vivekananda examines the creative nature and existence of man which, in his observation, is his religion in the expansion of human life. In this background he explains, "Thus, my religion means expansion, and expansion means realisation and perception in the highest sense - no mumbling words or genuflections. Man is to become divine, realising the divine more and more from day to day in an endless progress."[4] In this way the significance of this spiritual programme lies in the expansion of human existence which, according to Vivekananda, is the realisation and expression of the divine value through which man also becomes divine or spiritual. Thus, the proper meaning and significance of this idea of divinity is a synthesis of materiality and spirituality in the development of human existence, expanding the creative philosophy of Man, The Spiritual.

This philosophical programme of Swami Vivekananda contains the natural existence of man with its prospective development through the realisation of values in different directions, making the natural life and existence of man more creative and fruitful. As man exists in this material world, he has material demands of life. Mere satisfaction of these material interests, Vivekananda observes, produces limitation as the finiteness of life, responsible for creating contradictions as evils. In this context, it may be said that the significance of human existence lies not in material contradictions or evils only, but in the transcendence of evils through the expansion of goodness as the expression of potential perfection in man with the harmonisation of values for introducing unity in differences or contradictions. This, according to Vivekananda, is a spiritual development of materiality and spirituality with the expression of infiniteness or universality in human existence in different degrees for the realisation of the highest value of goodness as divine unity. This, in his observation, is the manifestation of God in man as the divinisation of man or Man, The Spiritual.

So God, in this spiritualistic process, has been taken as the central force of harmonising theistic, atheistic and absolutistic values, with a development of the creative unity of divinity and humanity in human existence. This spiritual programme of developing unity is examined by Vivekananda thus: "Their final essence is the teaching of unity. This, which we see as many, is God. We perceive matter, the world, manifold sensation. Yet there but one existence."[5] The significance of this 'one existence' lies in the development of God in human life as divine unity in plurality, expressing man's potential perfection in different degrees for the final realisation of unity as One or Self as Non-dual or Absolute.

This absolute state of existence, according to Swamiji, expresses the highest state of human freedom as a realisation of transcendent value of unity with the synthetic expressions in different experiential processes of developing unity in individual and social existence. For this synthetic programme of developing human freedom in unity, Vivekananda puts much importance on the humanistic processes of life which, in his observation, are disinterested process of love and unconditional service for mankind. These humanistic processes, according to Vivekananda, create a spirit of detachment or renunciation that inspires one to love and to work for others unconditionally which, according to Swamiji, "...is to love living beings, is to serve God." It may be recognised as the divinisation of man as the expression of the potential nature of love as perfection which unites man and God in a selfless process of love in service for others as the realisation of absolute value of love as perfect Bliss or *Anandam.* Through this unconditional and selfless process of manifesting absolute value, man realises his infinite nature, transcending different conditions or contradictions as finiteness with an expansion of potential unity or universality as human freedom as the unity of matter and spirit in human existence.

This is evaluated by Swami Vivekananda as a synthetic programme of expanding spirituality as the divinity of man is the non-duality of man and God or divinity and humanity which properly reveals the state of human freedom as a socio-spiritual unity of transcendent value of godness or divinity in an unconditional socio-moral process, reconciling social and moral contradictions.

Vivekananda evaluates this synthetic programme in a very natural way. The material demands of man in this worldly life, instigate him to satisfy his poor material interests. Vivekananda explains, "Then there is the desire to be happy. We run after everything to make ourselves happy; we pursue our mad career in the external world of senses."[6] Mere material desire for sensual pleasure or happiness, according to Vivekananda, creates contradictions between individual and collective or social interests which are responsible for producing social and moral evils. But the real nature of man, expressing his 'potential perfection,' inspires him to cross the limits of self-interests through the cultivation of the humanistic spirit for greater or wider social welfare of the people. In the analysis of this real human nature, Vivekananda points out, "The body is not the Real Man, neither is the mind, for the mind wakes and wanes. It is the Spirit beyond, which alone can live for ever."[7] The expansion of this spirit in human existence, manifests a selfless, disinterested feeling of oneness which develops a synthetic world view, cultivating a spirit of unity of man, god and world. This has been evaluated by Vivekananda as divinisation or spiritualisation which in one hand, engages man in disinterested service for others and on the other hand, it unites one with others unconditionally. It develops a spirit of universality when one feels his own existence in others and also knows others in him. In this synthetic process there is a development of final state of non-duality as a supreme state of human freedom. This may be evaluated as the humanistic process of developing non-duality or divine unity in human existence as human freedom.

In this background of the analysis of the spirituality as transcendent value of divine unity with its experiential programme for developing harmony in individual and collective or social existence, Vivekananda evaluates all thoughts and activities of human beings, experimented in different religions, cultures and philosophies of the world. In the synthetic and spiritual process, he observes the prospect of developing unity in all varieties and differences as the harmonisation of facts and truth, ways and opinions, life and ideals, men and communities. Vivekananda examines this possibility in a very natural manner, "Unity in variety is the plan of the universe. We are all men; and yet we are all distinct from one another. As a part of humanity I am one with you, and as Mr so-and-so I am different from you. As a man you are separate from the woman; as a human being you are all one with the Woman. As a man you are separate from the animal, but as living beings, man, woman, animal, and plant all are one; and as existence, you are one with the whole universe. That universal existence is God, the ultimate Unity in the Universe. In Him we are all one."[8] This is a spiritual process of developing transcendent or divine form of unity, through which Vivekananda explains the experiential programme of expressing harmony in human existence.

Thus, in this background, individual man, according to him, is a natural expression of perfection, developing unity as infiniteness or universality in his different state of existence. This essential process of expressing unity in different states of individual existence, manifests the state of universality in collective or social existence of man with the harmonisation of values and activities of human beings. These ideas of Vivekananda become fruitful and creative through the introduction of his ideal state which is a state of harmony of different communities in a society with the development of a state of equilibrium of their values or qualities and activities. This is a programme of introducing *Spiritual Socialism* in a transcendent-experiential background which is a democratic process of harmonising men in a natural way of evolving unity in their individual and collective existence. So it is not an artificial process of imposing unity on human existence from outside and for this Vivekananda, in his philosophy of *spiritual socialism* with the development of ideal state, emphasises the awakening of the proletariat or *shudras* with the essential character of proletariat as '*shudrahood*'. The social significance of this programme is not to develop a particular class for '*the dictatorship of proletariat*' as suggested by Marx. He, on the contrary, puts much importance on the essential development of *proletariat* or *shudra* class in harmony with values or qualities and activities of other classes or communities in a society. So in this socio-spiritual process there will not be the development of a particular system or class with the elimination of different values or qualities of other systems or classes. It, to the contrary, is a harmonious development of values and activities of different classes or communities in a society, for an essential advancement of social freedom in unity, making philosophy of integration on national level more creative with the introduction of a programme of unity in pluralities. Thus, it may be said that this integrated development of men or communities through the harmonisation of their values, overcoming limitations and differences, expand the idea of national value or social good, reconciling cultural contradictions or evils with an advancement of intercultural community *as* one nation.

In the analysis of this process, Vivekananda points out, "... what are nations but multiplied individuals? So, each nation has a mission of its own to perform in this harmony of races...."[9] Thus, it may be noted that in such a process of developing harmony, the life of individuals and the existence of nation as the collection of individuals become fruitful and significant.

In the same way if we explain the importance of social freedom in the international state of existence as the expansion of universality in individuals and communities, we shall find its completeness and effectiveness through the introduction of harmony among nations or cultures in an intercultural programme of developing integration which is nothing but an intercommunication of values, present in different nations or communities. In this process of developing harmony of nations or communities in an intercultural form, there is a prospect of developing World Unity through the reconciliation of differences of cultures or communities in the world.

In this intercultural programme of developing world unity, there is a prospect of developing World Community as prescribed by different political philosophers and sociologists, over the limitations and the contradictions, present in different communities. According to R.M. MacIver and Charles H. Page, "The wholly self-contained community belongs to the primitive world. In the modern world the nearest approach it is found in the huge nation-community included within the frontiers of a single State."[10] In this background they observe the present prospect of advancing world view with an expansion of the limits of several communities. They write thus, "We have noted the expansion of community to the dimension of the nation and, perhaps, the world."[11]

In this process, Vivekananda observes the intercommunication of ideas of different religions, cultures or communities with a prospective expansion of unity and universality. He writes, "The Bible, The Vedas, the Koran, and all other sacred books are but so many pages, and an infinite number of pages remain yet to be unfolded. I would leave it open for all of them. We stand in the present, but open ourselves to the infinite future. We take in all that has been in the past, enjoy the light of the present, and open every window of the heart for all that will come in the future."[12] Thus, in his observation, it is a natural and continuous process of unfoldment with an expansion of universal unity in different states, expressing the 'stage of perfection' as human freedom which he evaluates as 'the merging of the individual and the universal spiritual source.'

This process of merging of individuality and universality, according to Vivekananda, is a spiritual form of expanding unity in a well-organised way. It, in the observation of J.*S.* Mackenzie, a well known sociologist, is also to be 'characterised as spiritual unity.' Its significance in human life is evaluated by Mackenzie thus, is a kind of unity of which only spiritual beings-i.e. persons-would seem to be capable. Such beings are more or less clearly conscious of themselves as persons pursuing some good, and conscious of those with whom they are associated as other persons pursuing the same or a similar good."[13] This spiritual process of cultivating good in human existence, is a development of the humanistic relation of unity which makes the collective or social existence of man more significant and fruitful. Mackenzie again points out, "A well-ordered society is, in general, based upon a pretty clear consciousness of things to be pursued that are, in some degree, for the benefit of all; and it is at least safe to affirm that the more fully this is the case the more complete is the unity of the whole."[14] This form of 'unity of the whole' is a comprehensive form of developing the idea of transcendent value of unity with the different experiential processes of expressing it in human-existence in different degrees, making human life and activities more fulfilled.

This process of cultivating comprehensive attitude, according to Vivekananda, synthesises spiritualism and humanism, introducing a novel form of synthetic philosophy of man that develops practical and human outlook on the traditional and spiritual ways of *Upanishads* and *Vedanta*. This is a development of the transcendent divine value in the socio-cultural philosophy of *Humanism*. In this humanistic programme, Vivekananda, like Karl Marx, places man at the centre of history and also interprets human essence in expressing his freedom which is a pervasive process behind all orders of experience.

Thus, through the introduction of the spiritual form of humanistic order in the social, political, religious, cultural and other orders in general, Vivekananda emphasises the human freedom as the humanistic development with the natural and coherent expression of man as the religion of man. This process is a systematic development of the philosophy of man with an expansion of a new and a synthetic order of *Spiritual Humanism*. It is a change of anti-humanistic attitude with the introduction of universal humanistic spirit, making the individual and social existence of man more significant through the harmonious development of infinite personality of man as the coherent expression of his potential perfection with the manifestation of unity in different states of his existence. This may be evaluated as the socio-spiritual form of expressing and expanding divinity on earth.

This divine process of life and existence may also be treated by Vivekananda as process of *Yoga* or Union which is a spiritual process of transcending contradictions or evils with the introduction of unity as the divinised humanity or goodness as the reconciliation of evils. In this process, Vivekananda emphasises the four-fold *Yoga* of *Jnana. Karma, Raja* and *Bhakti* to divinity in unconditional love and service to humanity which, in the observation of R. Rolland, is a creative development of social equality and justice. In this humanistic process, emphasis is given upon unity in a natural process of love and service through which there will be an a wakening of all to a perfect condition-Eastern and Western.

The significance of these humanistic processes has been evaluated by Vivekananda, "Their final essence is the teaching of unity." Its expansion in human existence, is an expansion of human freedom which is evaluated by him in the following way. He writes, "However mistaken we may be as to the method, all our struggle is really for freedom. We seek neither misery nor happiness, but freedom. This one aim is the secret of the insatiable thirst of man. Man's thirst, says the Hindu, man's thirst, says the Buddhist, is a burning, unquenchable thirst for more and more. You Americans are always looking for more pleasure, more enjoyment. You cannot be satisfied, true; but at bottom what you seek is freedom. This vastness of his desire is really the sign of man's own infinitude. It is because he is infinite, that he can only be satisfied when his desire is infinite and its fulfillment infinite."[15]

So this type of humanistic philosophy of Vivekananda, evaluating the infiniteness in man with the expansion of his freedom in unity, makes him more prominent in contemporary Indian philosophy. Like all other contemporary Indian thinkers, he tries to examine the humanistic values, present in traditional Indian thoughts of *Vedas*, *Upanishads*, different systems of Indian philosophy, religion and culture. In this process he makes a comparative study of the East and the West for the development of a new form of *Humanism* as the religion of humanity in an intercultural context which is an expansion of divine unity in man as the development of Man, The Spiritual in a disciplined humanistic process.

In this process, man is placed to manifest his potential perfection in a gradual progress of his life towards the realisation and expression of the highest state of human existence as freedom in unity where there is a place for fostering a comprehensive attitude behind all restrictive consciousness in any religious, philosophical or cultural experience.

The manifestation of this comprehensive attitude in human life is nothing but the inauguration of unity or harmony in man and society. For the development of this state of unity or a common vibrant process-Rabindranath expresses it as a love of the transcendent infinity in its pursuit towards the finite, where beauty dwell-and life becomes tolerable inspite of its confronted sorrows and mishaps. Vivekananda, to achieve this comprehensive religious experience, prescribes several *Yogas* for the development of the potential power of man, ending up with a manifestation of a disciplined love and service for mankind for the realisation of perfection or divinity in man as God or Absolute. Sri Aurobindo also directs the supramental method of *Yoga* for establishing a process of divine union in man through a complete surrender to the transcendent divine process which is his supermind. Through these different methods, these three greats try to develop a comprehensive human outlook of religion and philosophy that is a harmonious progress in developing unity or harmony in life and society.

In this background the object of this work is to deal with the religious philosophy of Swami Vivekananda, evaluating his broad humanistic outlook, expressed through the religion or philosophy of human life and existence as the religion of man. Religion, according to him, is a process of becoming divine by some disciplined yogic process which will be indicated in the body of this work in their advanced developments and in terms of modem scientific methods. In this way the final object of the religion of man as advanced by Vivekananda, is not to avoid this life and world but to introduce a novel mode of doing divine service by serving man, relieving man of his miseries in organismic and socio-cultural processes due to man's ignorance.

The present work is divided into four chapters. Chapter 1 on "Swami Vivekanada: His Synthetic Programme for promoting the idea of Man, The Spiritual" with Part I: 'From individuality to Universality' and Part II: on 'Synthetic outlook about Man and World', deal with the life of Vivekananda with continuous advancement of his thought and outlook. In Indian tradition, thoughts are not divorced from the process of life. So philosophy is associated with activities. In this background, the object of the first chapter of this work, is to examine the coherent development of the humanistic thought and outlook of Swami Vivekananda through its expression and realisation in service for man, advancing his synthetic vision of Man, The Spiritual as the unity of spirituality or universality and humanity in human existence.

Chapter 2 on 'The Philosophical Significance of Man, The Spiritual: An Intercultural Development of the Religion of Humanity' contents two parts. Part I: on 'Religious, Scientific and Philosophical Prospects of Man and Part II: on 'Freedom in Unity in Tradition and Prospect'. These parts under chapter II, examines the philosophy of Man, The Spiritual in a religious and scientific background in explaining the natural and social significance of man in a-transcendent- experiential process as the religion of man with a proper cultivation of socio-spiritual value of humanity. This is a humanistic programme where there is a place for the development of a series of disciplined yogic ways to acquire divine power, by the practice of selfless love and service for mankind. This is a creative process of realising the state of human freedom as the manifestation of divine unity in human situation.

Chapter 3 on 'Swami Vivekananda's ideas and ideals: A Critical and Comparative Evaluation' contains two Parts. Part I: 'An Examination of Swamiji's Philosophy of Man and Part II: On 'The Philosophy of Spiritual Humanism' which are concerned with a critical and comparative study of the philosophy of Vivekananda that explains his uniqueness in developing the humanistic idea of religion towards the introduction of the philosophy of *Spiritual Humanism*.

Chapter 4 On 'Concluding Observations on Man, The Spiritual: An Intercultural Expansion of Swami Vivekananda's Synthetic Vision of Humanity', contains the concluding part 'Problems and Prospect of Swami Vivekananda's Intercultural Ideal, a Reality'. It deals with the concluding remarks on the entire discussion on Vivekananda's philosophy as the humanistic approach to religion and philosophy as the religion of man. It is intercultural in spirit with a prospect of expanding intercultural ideal, a reality.

It may finally be said that, this programme is an evaluation of man, manifesting his creative essence with a development of his dynamic nature, beyond any limited or static conception. Here lies the significance of spirituality that is the humanistic realisation of multidimensional potency of man as his creative infiniteness or divinity with its harmonious expression and dynamic development in individual and collective existence as unity in diversities. It is a socio-cultural programme of expanding integration- in an intercultural form for realising humanistic values, present in different men and in different nations or communities, as the harmonisation of individualities and universality, transcending limitations or contradictions. In this process of integration in an unconditional or disinterested form, there will be a creative development of unity of the humanistic idea of the East and the scientific outlook of the West, preparing an international ground for world peace. It, in the observation of Radhakrishnan, "...is the meaning of international understanding or human reconciliation."[16] In this process of reconciliation, the humanistic programme of Vivekananda expands the prospect of world unity. He observes, "A time must come when every man will be as intensely practical in the scientific world as in the spiritual, and then that Oneness, the harmony of Oneness, will pervade the whole world."[17]

Notes and References

1. P. Gisbert, S.I., *Fundamentals* of *Sociology,* 1959, p. 218.
2. *Ibid.,* p. 287.
3. 1.S. Mackenzie, *Outlines* of *Social Philosophy,* 1961, p. 209.
4. *Complete Works of Swami Vivekananda,* Birth Centenary Edition, 1963, Vol. I., p. 332.
5. *Ibid.* Vol. VIII. p. 250.
6. *Ibid.* Vol. II, p. 71.
7. *Ibid.* Vol. II, p. 79.
8. *Ibid.* Vol. ll, p. 381.
9. *Ibid.* Vol. II, p. 371.
10. R.M. Maclver and Charles H. Page. *Society,* 1962, pp. 10-11.
11. *Ibid.,* p. 11.
12. *Complete Works of Swami Vivekananda,* Birth Cent. Edn, 1963, Vol. II, p. 374.
13. Mackenzie, J.S., *Outlines of Social Philosophy,* 1961, p. 58.
14. *Ibid,* p. 59.
15. Unity, Notes of a lecture delivered at the Vedanta Society, New York, in June, *1900, Complete Works of Swami Vivekananda,* Birth Cent. Edn, 1963, Vol. VIII, p. 250.
16. S. Radhakrishnan, *The Creative Life,* Orient Paperbacks" 1975, p. 63.
17. *Complete Works of Swami Vivekananda,* Birth Cent. Edn, 1963, Vol. II, p. 188.

Chapter – 1

Swami Vivekananda: His Synthetic Programme for Promoting the Idea of Man, The Spiritual

Part - I

From Individuality to Universality

Indian Philosphy is closely related to the natural development of religious outlook of man as the Indian way of life that influences the contemporary Indian philosophy and Swami Vivekananda, like all other contemporary Indian philosophers, who wants to develop a complete view of religion that is one with philosophy on the basis of the proper explanation of life which comprehends the socio-cultural, political, economic and spiritual development of man in intercultural way. This prospective analysis of religion includes the human life which also finally stands on religion.

Vivekananda was a Vedantist in the advanced post-Buddhist current of Indian thought and was an Indian monk, so he did not deny the importance of life in the material world but lifted himself from it by detaching himself from all material concerns and disharmonies through the development of a search for an ideal religious attitude. He had a Vedantic attitude, viewing the confronted universe, mind, life and matter as non-different from *Brahman.*[1] Thus, the life of man, as Swamiji observes, is nothing but the manifestation of the transcendent divinity that makes him perfect above all material evils.

This view of man inspired Vivekananda to develop his religious philosophy which is the realisation of reality or perfection in man through disciplined love or *Bhakti Yoga*. But as perfection is potent in man, so according to Vivekananda, the development of the religious life of man is nothing but the manifestation of the yogic perfection of love and service to humanity as a whole. So the development of the philosophy of religion stands for a development of the perfection in human life in different degrees through different disciplined ways of Yogas-Jnana, *Karma, Raja* and *Bhakti,* the details of which will be found in the body of this work. His development of religious experience, is an interrelated process of discipline ranging from a basic consciousness *(Jnana)* to selfless activity or service *(Karma)* by a process of discipline in the eightfold ways from the control of the different parts of one's body, to the control of one's breath and mental process so as to rise beyond the wonderings of the mind and conserve energies *(Raja yoga)* and reverting them to the yoga of love *(Bhakti yoga*) by a continuous process of sacrifice and detachment.

The influence of different human qualities in developing his humanistic idea

In order to explain the proper nature of the broad human outlook of Vivekananda's philosophy of religion, we have to go through the sources and background of this human outlook and then we shall try to explain its development through the socio-cultural view that finally leads to the prospect of goal towards an ideal disciplined process of manifestation of Divine Love through service and total surrender of one's lower egoistic self.

The life of Vivekananda was as if a historical necessity as it becomes evident from his birth. He was born in the famous Dutta family of Calcutta on Monday, the 12th January,1863, when Indians were exploited under British rule. Vivekananda's message was also very much important in history. His was an inspiration for acquiring social freedom which presupposes one's freedom from self-centred mentality that finally leads one to the prospective attitude towards whole humanity. This has been evaluated by Bipin Chandra Pal, - "Vivekananda's message was really the message of modern humanity. His appeal to his own people was, 'Be men'."[2]

In the development of this broad human outlook with spiritual qualities, the well known Dutta family influenced him very much as he followed the ideals of his ancestors who "were noted for their liberal education and high standard of culture, unbounded charity and catholicity of outlook", and were under the guidance of the broad outlook of his father, who "spent of his ample earning without any thought of the morrow and as a result he could hardly store up and leave behind, till the end," any fortune for his family, and under the sympathetic training of his mother, "who was adorned with similar exemplary virtues." Vivekananda's mother like his father was idealistically oriented. Narendra (Vivekananda's early name) was inspired by her towards truthfulness from his early boyhood which became evident in his long life with his school friends. Different human qualities predominant in Dutta family developed the potentialities of the child Narendranath towards the great Swami Vivekananda, who inherited "such glorious traditions, would blossom forth in after years as one of the most powerful personalities destined to usher in an age of fresh glory for India and a new order of things for the world outside".[3] This became manifest from his school days. He was an extraordinary child.

Thus, in and through the family, school and college education, Narendranath came in contact with different personalities, books and ideals, that inspired him to develop selfless attitude, and disinterested feelings for others. After the untimely death of his father he became the only earning member of the family, so he had to pass through the strains of life, but he remained courageous, and completed his education and imbibed the advanced western outlook of life through science, philosophy, religion etc. But at the same time cherished the best of the Eastern outlook through the disinterested attitude of different personalities that he faced-specially Sri Ramakrishna. He through his mother's help had a good background of the *Ramayana, Mahabharata* and *Puranas,* self-less ideals of love and perfection in *Vedas; Upanishads* and the spirit of non-dual attitude of the *Vedanta* in the post-Buddhist process of Sri Ramakrishna. He evaluated Eastern ideal with a balance as he was conversant with the advanced knowledge of the Western view of science, that finally equipped him with the courage to challenge Sri Ramakrishna who claimed that he had experienced God or mother-goddess Kali in every moment of his life.

In this context it may be said that during his life he was very much influenced by the Indian spiritual experience of his time and by the disinterested way of life, as cultivated by his parents. His contact with his great master Sri Ramakrishna from time to time, before and after his father's death, transformed him gradually. Finally, after his father's death he became influenced by Sri Ramakrishna's way of life, and experimental way of confronting all types and orders of religious life, not of a scholar, but of an ordinary man, who claimed no scholarship by modesty and extreme innocence, but imbibed the essence of religious experience as developed from the *Vedas* and the *Upanishads* and *Tantras.* Sri Ramakrishna mastered the tantric experience through the help of Vairabi Brahmani, and the stringent Vedantic mystic experience of the impersonal *Brahman*, as transmitted to him by the itinerant monk, Totapuri, in almost no time. When left to himself he experimentally mastered the foreign religious experiences of the Islamic sufis and of Jesus Christ. With a purified exalted religious consciousness, Sri Ramakrishna "...lived to root out all distinctions between man and woman, the rich and the poor, the literate and the illiterate, Brahmans and the chandals...He came to bring about the synthesis of the Eastern and Western civilisations."[4] Swami Vivekananda, through a single touch of this master's direct experience of Mother Kali, was transformed to another world and developed a different vision of the confronted universe.

The Impact of his Great Master in awakening greatness in him

Narendranath met the great Master Sri Ramakrishna in such a time when his mind was full of problems about the nature of truth or reality. In the college days a scientific and rational outlook of Narendranath was developed through the influence of the contributions of the scientific thoughts of the West, as supplied by Darwin, Herbert Spencer, John Stuart Mill, Descartes, Hume and many other free thinkers. This outlook in Narendranath urged him to think against the superstitions of society and dogmatic view of Hindu life; that got much inspiration from the enlightened protest against dogmatism and orthodoxy of Hinduism from Brahmo Samaj, founded by Raja Rammohan Roy in 1828 A.D., Arya Samaj started by Swami Dayanand Saraswati in 1875 in Bombay and Theosophical Society founded by Madame Blavatsky in 1875. Thus, in this process, the rational and scientific thinking of Narendranath developed a truth seeking mind in him that inspired him to know and to realise the true nature of reality, which finally forced him to raise the most important question before Debendranath Tagore, "Sir, have you seen God?" He got no positive answer from Debendranath and when he met Sri Ramakrishna, he raised the same question again before him and Sri Ramakrishna confirmed, "Yes, I see Him just as I see you, only in a much intense sense. God can be realised; one can see and talk to Him as I am doing with you." Narendranath was surprised and then through a close contact with this great guru (which was a mystic touch by Sri Ramakrishna), he realised the unity of Joy, Light, Blessedness and Truth and thus all doubts or scepticism of Narendranath were removed and "Sri Ramakrishna…moulded him according to the ideal he had in mind, the ideal which became living and incarnate as the Swami Vivekananda."[5]

Swamiji learned from Sri Ramakrishna that God realisation is the essential feature of all religions and this realisation means the expression of the proper nature of man as the manifestation of divinity in man. Thus, the essence of religion lies in a transforming consciousness. To Sri Ramakrishna religious experience is a transforming experience and he observes, "As out of the same gold various ornaments are made having different forms and names, so our God is worshipped in different countries and ages, and has different forms and names. Though He may be worshipped variously, some lovingly call Him father, others mother, etc. yet it is one God that is being worshipped in all these various relations and modes."[6]

In this way the realisation of God in different relations and forms is nothing but the humanisation of God. It is realising God in man as 'I am God', -*'Aham Brahmasmi.'* According to Sri Ramakrishna, to see God in men and in all living beings, is knowledge and to see the world without God is ignorance. This view of Sri Ramakrishna inspired Swamiji to realise the non-dual view of *Advaita Vedanta*, -*'Jivo Brahmaiva naparah'*. So the existence of man is potentially divine that leads to the realisation of God in Man which is the fundamental end of religion of man as the humanisation of religion. Bipin Chandra Pal examines this process thus, -"To help man to realize his essential divinity is the object of all religious culture. This is what Vivekananda really meant when he appealed to his people to be men…"[7]

This outlook of religion removes the evils of dogmatism and develops a democratic view towards unity and harmony as preached by Sri Ramakrishna through his teachings of '*Yata mat tata path*' or many minds many ways. He said, "I have practiced all religions, Hinduism, Islam, Christianity, and I have found that it is the same God towards whom all are, directing their steps, though along different paths. You must try all beliefs and traverse all the different ways. Where ever I look I see men quarrelling in the name of religion. Hindus, Mohammedans, Brahmos, Vaisnavas and the rest, but they never reflect that He, who is called Krishna is called Shiva, and bears the name of primitive Energy, Jesus and Allah, as well- the same Rama with a thousand names. The tank has several ghats. At one the Hindus draw water in pitchers and call it *jala;* at another Mussalmans draw water in leather bottles and call it *pani;* at the third Christians call it water, can we imagine that the water is not jala, but only pani or water? How ridiculous! The substance is one under different names and everyone is seeking the same substance.[8] This democratic view of Sri Ramakrishna accepts all religious values and remove all contradictions of different religions through the introduction of oneness in differences, because God or Ultimate Reality as the one or non-dual existence exists in everything and God also as the highest value, can be realised through disinterested love and service for humanity.

This wider, liberal and prospective integral outlook of religion supplied by Sri Ramakrishna inspired Vivekananda to accept religion through the disciplined process of love and service to mankind. Swami Vivekananda observed the development of these human values as nothing but the development of philosophy by a transformed vision, through the yogic disciplines finally rising from their consciousness to a developed process of manifestation of love and service to mankind, discovering divinity in man.

He writes: "The God is here before thee now,
Revealed in all these myriad forms;
Rejecting them, where seekest thou
His presence? He who freely shares
His love with every living thing
proffers true service unto God"[9]

To love God is to love 'every living beings,' that can be practiced through the development of the feeling of detachment, renunciation, and disinterestedness which can be proved by love and work for others. So the fundamental end of Vivekananda's religion is to establish religion on love and service to mankind as in this religious devotion to God precedes social service. This approach to God through the disciplined ways of love and service is a unique contribution of Swami Vivekananda, in his contemporary social milieu.

The social significance of this programme as suggested by Swami Vivekananda, is explained by Acharya Vinoba Bhave in the following way, "He, therefore advised us to dedicate ourselves to the service of '*Daridranarayana*' (God manifested in the hungry, destitute millions) to their upliftment and edification. The word '*Daridranarayana*' was coined by Vivekananda and popularised by Gandhiji.[10]

This social and human outlook of religion develops the spirit of saint in Swamiji that urges him to accept the philosophy of life of the Hindu Monk - a person dedicated to love and service. It is to be noted in this connection that Swamiji accepted this way of life not for ignoring this life and material world, but to overcome the apparent contradictions of this world from a materialist egoist attitude. His was a selfless and disinterested attitude towards life that opens the door of a new world of religion where he enters into the intrinsic nature of man and discovers that the causes of sorrows and sufferings lie in one's concentration on one's egoist self and attachment for material possessions.

So the influence of Guru Sri Ramakrishna on Vivekananda makes him a Man in a superior sense. He becomes-Man the Great. He learns from his great master that type of religion which is the expression of the true nature of man by disciplined ways, and so transformed, a man stands for the welfare of the people.

The idea of God in religion is the central force that leads man to feel his oneness with God. The development of man as Man the Great, through different selfless activities for others, is the manifestation of divinity in man. 'This idea raises the feeling of identity with others as each individual manifests divinity and that urges him to accept the sorrows and sufferings of others as his own. This is the introduction of man's oneness with others that finally reflects the ideal, -'*Jivo Brahamiva naparah*'. Man and God (or Absolute) are non-different, so the service of man is the service of God. For this Vivekananda writes in a poem, 'who loves the living beings, serves God.'[11] So to love and work for others is to develop man as Man, or God in him. All these ideas regard the non-duality between God and Man. It is a discovery, and a readiness for action or service to Man, as another open prospect for mankind.

From Narendranath, a man, to Swami Vivekananda, The Man

Through close contact with Sri Ramakrishna, Narendranath realised him as a perfect man with human qualities that influenced Naren very much, and the teaching of this great master helped him to understand that the existence of God in the form of *Sakara* or *Nirakara* is the adherence to an abstract problem. The real and advanced pursuit towards religious consciousness, lies in a yogic pursuit where disciplined knowledge and action rise to the comprehensive disciplined orders of love and service for mankind as a whole. Narendranth started an application of this process in his own life and in society.

As man exists in this material world he cannot ignore the reality of the worldly problems; he, on the other hand, can overcome them finally, by accepting them as confronted experiences. This gives a meaning to his functioning with love and serve mankind. After the death of his father on 25th February, 1884, Narendra also was bound to face different domestic troubles, and acute financial crisis that forced him to come to Sri Ramakrishna for begging money. Sri Ramakrishna told him to pray for himself to Divine Mother Kali at Daksineswar. But when he stood before Goddess Kali, he realised that his own sufferings were nothing much important if compared with the sufferings of many other persons. So he forgot his material demands and prayed for knowledge, devotion, renunciation and love for the development of a disinterested feeling for others.

In this process Narendranath realised the humanistic influence of his Master through the cultivation of a selfless sprit in him. C. Isherwood writes, "throughout the rest of his life, Naren would say frequently, Ever since our first meeting, it was the Master alone who always had faith in me-no one else, not even my own mother and brother. That faith and that love of his have bound me to him for ever. The master was the only one who knew how to love and who really loved. Worldly people only feign love to gratify their own self-interest."[12]

So, in this way in a selfless manner, Narendranath gradually learned the process of freedom from sufferings of all worldly people that inspired him to realise the inner significance of the Vaisnava religion, as interpreted by his great master-'It is not the sympathy to the creatures-but to serve all living beings as Siva or God'. This ideal of the service to man inspired Narendranath to overcome his domestic and worldly problems through the realisation of the freedom of men in and through the service to mankind as the ideal of humanity is nothing but the manifestation of the ideal of Divinity as Truth, Beauty and Goodness. This acceptance of an attitude towards life is not a mere idea, softly entertained, it has to be cultivated with a discipline. This cultivation as a new discipline is given later in this work.

Thus, through a disciplined method of the ideals of knowledge, love and service or in the process of *Sadhana* in the context of India's traditional background-young Narendranath gradually prepared himself as a transformed and perfect man and then with this acquired power, he organised a group of young disciples termed "*Sannyasi Sangha*" (organisation of the *Sannyasins* or detached people) according to the direction of his great master. He was to reach perfection under the ideal of disciplined love and service, where the object of worship was the suffering persons. Sri Ramakrishna had this ideal, Vivekananda gave it a practical shape. After the death or *mahasamadhi* of Sri Thakur on August 16,1886, Narendranath translated the human outlook of his great master into action and founded Sri Ramakrishna Math at Baranagar for the establishment of "the Sri Ramakrishna brotherhood for self-liberation as also for the well-being of humanity at large."[13]

This could be possible through selfless service to mankind. His was changed meaning given to liberation, as inherited from the past. In Baranagar Math, Narendranath with his other *gurubhais* (brothers in faith under the same teacher, Sri Ramakrishna developed a human and wider view of life under the practice of hardship in poverty. Narendranath explained before them 'the great books of human thought' and evaluated 'the-evolution of the universal mind' , from a discursive to practical attitude.

He had practical outlook and Sri Ramakrishna was a pointer in this direction. It is a descent from a transcendent consciousness to a confronted consciousness - the sphere of human sufferings. It was to be faced, but it had to be overcome, not theoretically but practically pointing out the divinity - in the confronted orders of the expression of love and selfless service. This selfless ideal inspired them to discard the former way of life by changing, one's past names, which prescribed their different lines of actions as suggested by their names. It was a concrete performance of *Virajahoma,* in the 3rd week of January, 1887. This process of life or *'sannyasa':* Its ideal and practice makes an individual to become the disciplined man, Swamiji explains this as below: "Those of you who are *sannyasins* must try to do good to others, for *Sannyasa* means that. There is no time to deliver a long discourse on "Renunciation", but I shall very briefly characterise it as "the love of death". Worldly people love life. The Sannyasin is to love death. Are we to commit suicide then? Far from it. For suicides are not lovers of death, as it is often seen that when a man trying to commit suicide fails, he never attempts it for second time. What is the love of death then? We must die, that is certain; let us die then for a good cause....There is no good in doing that unless you hold it also as a sacrifice to the whole world. For the world is one; you are rated a very insignificant part of it, and therefore it is right for you that you should serve your millions of brothers rather than aggrandise this little self."[14]

It is in a way acceptance of the Buddhist ideal of the dissolution of all intellectual propensity. In a sense, it is the love of death as a choice not to discuss which is the urge of ordinary indisciplined persons, who cherish worldly cravings. *Sannyasi* loves death, in that life of dedication to serve others, conscious of their miseries. Death is that to realise a higher mode of life, quitting the past mode and to get rid of selfishness or narrow interests, and to exist by serving others, which is real life for the good of others. Thus, through the practice of this ideal of Sannyasa, Narendranath became a great Hindu Monk of India, who after several changes of names, finally took the name Vivekananda. According to the opinion of his chief disciple, Maharaja of Khetri, Vivekananda proved himself a great revolutionary by his dynamic thought and action. His was a march towards the removal of the sufferings of human beings as a whole. In cherishing this ideal for the world he became rightly known as Swami Vivekananda, whose decision of this sort; was indeed a joy for ever.

Expansion of the universal feeling for man and mother land

Now, after the acceptance of the life of a *Sannyasi* or the life of renunciation, Vivekananda wanted to visit India for discovering the eternal spirit of India in and through the ways of common life. For this he accepted the life of *paribrajaka* for observing and realising the eternal spirit of unity in India and Indians. In 1888, Vivekananda as *paribrajaka* visited Ajodhya, Lakhnau, Varanasi. Brindabana, Agra, Hrisikesa etc.; in 1890 Varanasi, Gajipur, Allahabad and on 3rd August,1890, he started again and visited Vaidyanath, Bhagalpur, Nainital, Almora, Delhi, Meerut, Rajputana and different places of Western India and South India. In this long visit to different places of India, Swamiji came in contact with the life of man in different stages, common men, kings and queens, scholars, social reformers etc, that inspired him to learn India's own way of life on renunciation, tolerance and love. R. Rolland points out, "He wandered free from plan, caste, home, constantly alone with God. And there was no single hour of his life when he was not brought into contact with the sorrows, the desires, the abuses and feverishness of living men, rich and poor, in town and field; he became one with their lives, the great Book of Life revealed to him what all the books in the libraries could not have done,..."[15] This meeting with the different people of different sections inaugurated in Vivekananda a feeling of oneness with the life of Indians, that ultimately overwhelmed him with anxieties of sorrows and sufferings of men due to social inequalities, exploitation and injustice, which finally revealed to him"...the tragic face of the present day, the God struggling in humanity, the cry of the people of India and of the world for help and the heroic duty of the new Oedipus, whose task it was to deliver Thebes from the talons of the Sphinx or to perish with Thebes."[16]

This new revelation in Vivekananda inspired him to realise the philosophy of man as the religion of life that helps him to introduce the religion of man, that puts an importance on the existence of man as such, and the superiority of his existence against all exploitations and injustice that finally leads to the development of unity in human beings through the awakening of humanistic outlook as the spirit of equality. For the development of this outlook, Swamiji observed that the life and activities of each Indian are to be related to the eternal spirit of India. Vivekananda wrote, "Each nation has a main current in life, in India it is religion. Make it strong and the waters on either side must move along with it."[17] He thought that the only way to awake the self-forgetful Indian is to make him conscious about his existence as man with infinite possibilities, which stands on his spirit of religion, as it 'is the manifestation of the divinity'. This view relates a man with his cultural heritage which in the observation of Julian Huxley is "...the fuller realisation of more possibilities by the human species collectively and more of its component members individually."[18] The 'realisation of more possibilities' in this context, may be treated as the cultivation of the spirit of the divinised humanity which finally expands the idea of the *'Spiritual Humanism'* which is the development of socio-spiritual outlook as godness in man. Vivekananda points out, "You may invent an image through which to worship God, but a better image already exists, the living man. You may build a temple in which, to worship God, and that may be good, but a better one, a much higher one, already exists, the human body."[19] The opening of this idea of God in man leads to the well-being of all human beings on the basis of equality which is evaluated by Vivekananda thus, "Above all I believe in my God the wicked, my God the miserable my God the poor of all races." This leads to the socio-spiritual idea of unity which is explained by Swamiji, "A nation in India must be a union of those whose hearts beat to the same spiritual tune".

This 'spiritual tune' in the heart of man, expresses the inner essence of religion as revolving round man. This idea inspires Vivekananda to establish religion on human life and society which leads to spiritual renaissance in the country. Swamiji thinks this type of Renaissance precedes revolution. The significance of this religious process as the expression of divinity in man lies in the reconciliation of disunities or differences that inspires him to stand against all types of exploitations. In this background if we explain the history of the national movement in India we shall observe the creative influence of this idea that leads to the political revolution against the exploitations under British rule. It may be said thus that Vivekananda's revolutionary outlook of religion introduced a new form of *Religious Nationalism* in India on the basis of the feeling of the dignity of own country, reawakening of *Hinduism* and the development of Indian *spiritualism*.[20] Its importance on the national history has been evaluated by Ramesh Chandra Majumdar in the following way. He writes, "Swami Vivekananda thus gave a spiritual basis to Indian nationalism. The lessons of the *Vedanta* and *Bhagvad-Gita* permeated the lives and activities of many nationalists, and many martyrs, inspired by his teachings, endured extreme sufferings embraced death, and calmly bore the inhuman tortures, worse than death..."[21]

In the background of this historical importance of Vivekananda, supplying "spiritual basis to Indian nationalism", it is found that his fundamental object in this process was to cultivate the prospective revolutionary spirit in the traditional outlook and ways of the country. So it may be treated as the humanistic programme of associating national consciousness with the revolutionary activities for an introduction of the religion of humanity, expanding *Revolutionary Nationalism*. Its meaning, as Vivekananda observes, is the awakening of man as the expansion of his religion of life with the political, economic, social and spiritual development as humanistic freedom. Its significance lies in the change of individual and collective existence as the expansion of humanity through the change of limitations and contradictions out of dominations and exploitations.

In the analysis of the historical development of this humanistic programme in Bengal it may briefly be stated that *Hindu Mela*, introduced by Acharya Raj Narayan Basu, *Brahmo Samaj*, founded by Raja Rammohan Roy, *Sanjivani Sabha* of Jyotirindranath, *Sivaji Utsav* of Sakharam and other religio-social performances, cultivated a national consciousness which was expanded as *Nationalism* through the writings of Bankimchandra, Hemchandra, Nabinchandra, Bhudeb Mukhopadhyay, Sakharam Ganesh Deuskar and other nationalist writers and thinkers.

This idea of *Nationalism* became revolutionary in spirit and activity under the stimulating influence and guidance of Vivekananda who synthesised religion with life, expanding the humanistic idea of *Religious Nationalism*.

Thus, in this socio-religious process it is found that Bankim Chandra revived Sanatan Hindu religion (traditional *Hinduism*) through the circulation of *'Naba-Hinduvada'*, (New *Hinduism*) which was extended by Swami Vivekananda as *Religious Nationalism* with an expansion of religious ideas with values of national and social equality and justice. The synthesis of religion with *Nationalism* became clearer to Sri Aurobindo, another Acharya or a preceptor of the freedom movement in Bengal, who wrote "Nationalism is religion that has come from God."[22]

This has been evaluated by Vivekananda as a socio-spiritual process manifesting divinity and humanity in social and political freedom. This revolutionary spirit of Swamiji stimulated the Indian Nationalists and all of them accepted him as *'Jatiya Veera'* (National Hero). In 1900-01, Sister Nivedita, the disciple of Swami Vivekananda, joined the National Council for directing revolutionary work and delivered lectures in different places for awakening of the revolutionary spirit in young mind. The lecture on *'Dynamic Religion'* delivered by her in the Town Hall, was treated by Bipin Chandra Pal, an extremist, as '*Dynamite*'.[23] Thus, the introduction of humanistic religion in *Nationalism* by Vivekananda, inspired his followers very much. Its influence on the freedom fighters urged them to accept Vivekananda "to be more a political prophet than a religious teacher."[24] The fundamental principle of the *Religious Nationalism* created a new spirit in the national movement of India that gave birth to the act of freedom fighting. Regarding the nature of this active movement the remark of Bipin Chandra Pal is very much significant. He writes, "The fundamental point of difference between the older political agitations and the new Nationalist Movement is thus (1) its intensely spiritual and religious character as compared to the absolutely secular spirit of the former and (2) its strong grip in the activities of Indian life and thought against the imitative character of the older and earlier social and political activities."[25]

In the background of this analysis of Sri Pal it may be said that Vivekananda's attempt to reconcile religion with *Nationalism* is to develop national and spiritual outlook in man that helps him to be free from weakness, fear of death and other ordinary bondages of common life and also develops a greater self for others through love and service for justice and equality. This view of *Spiritualism* inspired Netaji Subhas Chandra Bose, another follower of Swamiji and well known freedom fighter, who in his young life, was habituated to recite Vivekananda's *'Kali the Mother'*.[26]

For Terror is Thy name
Death is in Thy breath,
And every shaking step
Destroys a world for e'er
Thou "Time', the All-Destroyer!
Come, O Mother, come
Who dares misery love
And hug the form of Death,
Dance in Destruction's dance,
To him the Mother comes.[27]

The inner significance of this poem lies in a spiritual process of destroying evils or contradictions with an external creation of good in life and existence. In this context it may be said that to go through the spiritual meaning of life means to inaugurate the human outlook or greater feeling for others through the suppression of poor ego or narrow self contradictions. This expanding spiritual process brought the '*spiritual renaissance*' through the development of "man-making religion" that changed the socio-political and cultural life of Indians, when Vivekananda declared boldly, "Our life-blood is spirituality. If it flows clear, if it flows strong and vigorous, everything is right;

political, social, any other material defects, even the poverty of the land..."[28]

So, the development of *Spiritualism* with its relation to *Nationalism*, establishes the fundamental principle of Vivekananda's religion of man i.e. firstly, the free existence of man in the society as the political freedom of Indians against British Rule; secondly, free existence of man above all material contradictions as disunity and disharmony caused by social injustice and inequality and lastly the introduction of social unity or harmony through the expansion of humanity.

In '*The Philosophy of Vivekananda and the Future of Man*', Gobinda Chandra Dev evaluated this process of expanding humanity in man and society. In his observation, Vivekananda, in this humanistic process, wanted to bring "the equilibrium between warring forces of life: reason and faith, matter and spirit, individual and society, science and religion, the past and the present, the East and the West, and last but not the least, haves and have-nots."

In this process, we find the expansion of a programme of harmonising divinity and humanity for an essential development of unity as the reconciliation of contradictions. This in the observation of Netaji Subhas Chandra Bose, is a synthetic process through which "Swamiji harmonised East and West, Religion and Science, past and present."[29] For this Netaji accepted Swamiji as the real guide and interpreter of Indian thought and Indian way of life. He wrote, "and that is why he is great. Our countrymen have gained unprecedented self-respect, self-confidence and self-assertion from his teachings".[30]

His teachings expanded the national outlook, cultivating a wider and humanistic feeling for men and motherland. This has been evaluated by Brahmabandhav Upadhayay with reference to the influence of Swami Vivekananda on his own life and activities. He explained this in the following way, "Swamiji! I was your friend in youth...But then I never knew that there was a lion's strength in your soul, a volcanic pain and passion for India in your heart. Today with all my humble strength I have come to follow your way...In the midst of this fierce struggle, whenever I get torn and tossed, whenever despondency comes overwhelms my heart, I look up to the great ideal you set forth, I recollect your leonine strength, meditate on the profound depths of your agony-then all at once my weariness withers away. A divine light and a divine strength comes from somewhere and fulfils my mind and heart."[31]

This, type of influence of Vivekananda with '....a divine light and a divine strength....', cultivated a proper humanistic outlook for an enrichment of Indian tradition and culture. This, according to Romain Rolland, paved the way for "greater India" which, in the observation of Swamiji, developed a "Vision of a new India,....the land where humanity has attained its highest towards gentleness, above all the land of introspection and of spirituality."[32]

This enlightened vision expanded through the neo-evaluation of the eternal spirit of his own motherland as "The land of introspection and of spirituality", opened the door of a new world where he wanted to realise the total existence of man in and through the worldly affairs. The significance of this realisation lies in the reconciliation of worldly contradictions in unity in human existence as the development of intrinsic eternity or spirituality in man.

In this spiritual meaning of human existence, Vivekananda examined the national spirit of India with a prospect of expanding universality as the harmonious development of divinity and humanity in this life and world. In this spirit, Swamiji thus emphasised, "I shall not cease to work. I shall inspire men everywhere, until the world shall know that it is one with God". The significance of this oneness lies in the unity of humanisation in the worldly existence.

Notes and References

1. *Brahma Satyam ...Jivo Brahmaiva naparah.*
2. *Prabuddha Bharat,* July, 1932, pp. 323-25.
3. R.C. Majumdar (Ed), *Swami Vivekananda Centenary Memorial Volume,* 1963, p. 34.
4. Swami Jagadananda (Tr), *Sri Rsmskrishne- The Great Master* by Swami Sharadananda, 2nd Edition, 1952, p. XI.
5. *Life of Swami Vivekananda: His Eastern and Western Disciples* 1974, p. 115.
6. Max Muller, *Ramakrishna-His Life and Sayings,* 1951, p. 162.

7. *Prabuddha Bharat,* July, 1932.
8. Swami Nikhilananda, *The Gospel of Sri Ramakrishna,* (English Translation) 1974, p. 480.
9. Swami Nikhilananda: *Vivekananda-A Biography,* (1st Ed.) 1953, p. 72.
10. *Prabuddha Bharat,* May, 1963, pp. 172-73.
11. Bahurupe Sammukhe tomar, chari kotha ksnujicha Isvar? Jive prern kare jei jan, sei jan sebiche Isvar.
12. Christopher Isherwood, *Ramakrishna and His Disciples,* 1980, p. 216.
13. Swami Vivekananda and His Message, *Swami Vivekananda Centenary Memorial Volume,* 1963, p. 57.
14. Swami Vivekananda, 'Sannyasa: Its ideal and Practice', *Complete Works of Swami Vivekananda,* Birth Centenary Edition, 1963, Vol. III, p. 446.
15. Romain Rolland: *The Life of Vivekananda and the Universal* Gospel, 1979, p. 21.
16. *Ibid.,* p. 21.
17. *Complete Works of Swami Vivekananda,* Birth Cent. Edition, 1963. Vol. IV. p. 373.
18. Swami Ranganathananda, *The Essence of Indian Culture,* 1966, pp. 22-23.
19. *Complete Works* of *Swami Vivekenende;* Birth Cent. Edition, 1963, Vol, II, p. 313.
20. Suprakas Roy, *Bhsretet Vaiplabik Sangramer ltihss,* 1970, Vol. I, p. 128.
21. R.C. Majumdar, *History of the Freedom Movement in India,* 1962,-Vol. I, pp. 358-63.
22. Speeches, *Sri Aurobindo,* Vol. I. Birth Centenary, Library, Pondicherry, 1972, p. 652.
23. S.N. Chattopadhyay, 'Viplabee Bangia', *Smarak Grantha,* Dum Dum Vidyut Chakra Sadharan Pathagar, pp. 10-11.
24. H. C. Ghosh, *Patriot-Prophet,* 1954, p. 335.
25. B. C. Pal, *The Spirit of Indian Nationalism,* 1910, p. 29.
26. Dilip Kumar Roy, *Smriti Charan;* 1367 B. S. p. 367.
27. Vivekananda, 'Kali, The Mother', *Complete Works of Swami Vivekananda,* Birth Centenary Edition, 1963, Vol. IV, p. 384.
28. *Complete Works* of *Swami Vivekananda,* Birth Cent. Edition, 1963, Vol. III, p. 288.
29. Swami Lokeswarananda and others (ed), *World Thinkers on Ramakrishna-Vivekananda,* 1983, p. 47.
30. *Ibid.*
31. Sankari Prasad Basu, *Vivekananda O Samakalin Bharatvarsha;* Vol. I, 1982, p. 351. (E.T., World Thinkers on Ramakrishna-Vivekananda, 1983, pp. 38-39).
32. *Complete Works of Swami Vivekananda,* Almora, 1918, Vol. III, p. 460.

Part - II

Synthetic Outlook about Man and World

The awakening of this wider view about the world inspired Swamiji to accept the practical reality of this world and worldly life that urged him to establish the principle of his religion of man in this life when he understood, "Religion is not for empty bellies." Without the material body in this world, man cannot go through the essence of spirituality; so firstly, he should assert his existence in this material world. This view of Vivekananda about the practical reality of the material existence of man seized him with anxiety of poverty of his countrymen, who were to be well fed, clothed and sheltered. So he thought to go through the art of material prosperity of the West and wanted to develop the material existence of Indians on the basis of the material support from the West. At the same time, he also wanted to develop the material outlook of the Western thought and culture through the inauguration of universal humanistic outlook, supplied by the eternal religion on Indian spiritualism. This worldly process may be evaluated as the humanistic programme of Vivekananda which is explained by Christopher Isherwood in the following way. He wrote, "Vivekananda looked towards the West, not simply as a mass of tyrants exploiting various parts of Asia, and other undeveloped areas, but as future partners, people who had very, very much to offer. At the same time, without any false humility, he faced the West and said, "We have fully as much and more to offer you. We offer you this great tradition of spirituality, which can produce, even now, today, a supremely great figure such as Ramakrishna. You can offer us medical services, trains that run on time, hygiene, irrigation, electric light.

These are very important, we want them, and we admire some of your qualities immensely".[1] Thus, through an inter-change of thought and culture, materialism and spiritualism, he finally wanted to develop unity and interrelation between the East and the West. Nivedita observed on this programme, "a double purpose is served, one of world-moving, and another, of nation-making."[2]

When Swamiji was thinking in this manner, he, at that time, heard that the Parliament of Religions was going to be held at Chicago and he at once thought to be present there for the inauguration of the voice and spirit of man in this *Parliament* of the world. This desire of Swamiji was fulfilled by the common people of India as they collected money to send Vivekananda to America[3] and on 31st May, 1893, he embarked the ship in Bombay and started on his remarkable journey towards the world, anew. The object and the activity of Vivekananda in this programme for visiting America, is examined by Sri Aurobindo thus, "The visit of Swami Vivekananda to America and subsequent work of those who followed him did more for India than a hundred London congresses could effect that is the true way of awakening sympathy, by showing ourselves to the nations as a people with a great past and ancient civilisation who still possesses something of the genius and character of our forefathers, have still something to give the world and therefore deserve freedom,-by proof of our manliness and fitness, not by mendicancy."[4] In the background of this observation of Sri Aurobindo, it may be pointed out that Vivekananda with genius and character visited different places and met different men, communicating his humanistic spirit for freedom.

During the journey, he visited Colombo in Ceylon, a seat of Buddhist culture, Penang, Singapore, Hong Kong; Canton, the then capital of China, and then went to Osaka; Yokohama, Nagasaki, Kyoto, Tokyo and different industrially advanced cities of Japan and was very much delighted to go through the modem development of life on the basis of a synthesis of culture of the East and the West. In this way he reached Vancouver in British Columbia on 25th July and from there he reached Chicago on 30th July, by train. During this period Swamiji met many distinguished scholars and discussed different subjects with them. Thus, he came in contact with Mr J. H. Wright,

Professor of Harvard University who was influenced by the deep scholarship of Swamiji and discovered the ability and the versatility of genius of a great man in this Hindu Monk. This inspired Mr Wright to introduce Vivekananda before the selection committee of delegates and wrote a letter to his friend, the chairman of the committee, where he emphasised, "Here is a man who is more learned than all our learned professors put together."

Thus, Vivekananda got the entry to the *Parliament of Religion* in the Hall of Columbus at the Art Institute of Chicago, which started on 11th September, 1893 at 10 am with the representations of different important religions of the world like *Hinduism, Buddhism, Mahammedanism, Theism, Judaism, Zoroastrianism, Confucianism, Taoism, Shintoism, Protestantism, the Greek Church, Catholicism* etc.

This *Parliament* will be remembered for ever not for the representations of different religions of the world but for the introduction of the humanistic idea of unity among all men of all religions through the inauguration of *Universal Humanism* in religion. This was introduced by Swami Vivekananda, a Hindu monk of India and in his address when he invited common men to open their inner spirit of unity with its communication through the words '*Sisters and Brothers of America*.' After the utterance of these delightful words, Dr Barrows, the Chairman of the selection committee of delegates, pointed out, 'there arose a peal of applause that lasted for several minutes' and the entire audience got much inspiration from him and their inner urge increased more and more when he interpreted the idea of God as the spirit of unity as one truth in men of all religions: "As the different streams having their sources in different places, all mingle their water in the sea, so, O Lord, the different paths which men take through different tendencies, various though they appear, crooked or straight, all lead to Thee."[5] This spiritual outlook of unity in men was explained by Swamiji in a more scientific manner when he discussed the nature of the object of science and religion as nothing but to reach, the Unity in diversity: "Science is nothing but the finding of unity. As soon as science would reach perfect unity, it would stop from further progress, because it would reach the goal. Thus, chemistry could not progress further when it would discover one element out of which all others could be made. Physics would stop when it would be able to fulfill its services in discovering one energy of which all the others are but manifestations, and the science of religion becomes perfect when it would discover Him, who is the one life in a universe of death, Him who is the constant basis of an ever-changing world-one who is the only soul of which all souls are but delusive manifestations. Thus, is it, through multiplicity and duality, that the ultimate unity is reached. Religion can go no further. This is the goal of all science."[6]

After the interpretation of the religious and scientific outlook of truth as unity, Vivekananda pointed out that its fundamental basis is in the human nature which tries to realise and express it in different stages of life in different degrees. Vivekananda evaluates this process in the following manner. He writes, "…man is not travelling from error to truth, but from truth to truth, from lower to higher truth. To him all the religions, from the lowest fetishism to the highest absolutism, mean so many attempts of the human soul to grasp and realise the Infinite, each determined by the conditions of its birth and association, and each of these marks a stage of progress; and every soul is a young eagle soaring higher and higher, gathering more and more strength, till it reaches the Glorious Sun."[7]

Thus, in the observation of Vivekananda, unity in differences, expressing human truth is the basic feature of man and society. But the difficulty of a particular religion or philosophy is to place men and society under certain fixed dogmas that create contradictions. This dogmatic outlook of religion and philosophy is to be removed through the development of the humanistic spirit of unity as truth that, according to Swamiji, is also an essential feature of *Hinduism* as religion of life and culture. He explains "Unity in variety is the plan of nature, and the Hindu has recognised it. Every other religion lays certain fixed dogmas, and tries to force society to adopt them. It place before society only one coat which must fit Jack and John and Henry, all alike. If it does not fit John or Henry, he must go without a coat to cover his body. The Hindus have discovered that the absolute can only be realised, or thought of, or stated through the relative; and the images, crosses, and crescents are simply so many symbols-so many pegs to hang the spiritual ideas on."[8]

In the background of this analysis of the Hindu view of life as the realisation of unity in men in society, Vivekananda points out that this type of humanistic spirit in unity leads to the development of the ideal of Universal Religion of Man through the expansion of humanity which, according to him, is the proper expression of the spirituality in human existence as the unfoldment of universality as divinity in man as Man, The Spiritual. He explains this process in the following manner: "...If there is ever to be a universal religion, it must be one which will have no location in place or time; which will be infinite like the God it will preach, and whose sun will shine upon the followers of Krishna and of Christ, on saints and sinners alike; which will not be *Brahminic* or *Buddhistic*, Christian or Mohammedan, but the sum total of all these, and still have infinite space for development;...It will be a religion which have no place for persecution or intolerance in its polity, which will recognise divinity in every man and woman, and whose whole scope, whose whole force will be centred in aiding humanity to realise its own true, divine nature."[9] In this context of the analysis of the universality in human existence, Vivekananda examines the idea of religion as the evaluation of the infinite nature of man as the synthetic expression of divinity as humanity. This, in the observation of Vivekananda, is nothing but the expression of the ideal of *Humanism* in the Universal Religion of Man that finally inspires man to develop his human qualities for the realisation of unity or harmony beyond all disunities and contradictions, created out of religious dogmas. Thus, in the concluding session of the Parliament of Religion, Vivekananda explained the social significance of the universality introduced in the Parliament for the development of synthetic and humanistic outlook of religion as the realisation of man. He observes, "if the Parliament of Religions has shown anything to the world it is this: It has proved to the world that holiness, purity, and charity are not the exclusive possessions of any church in the world, and that every system has produced men and women of the most exalted character. In the face of this evidence, if anybody dreams of the exclusive survival of his own religion and the destruction of the others, I pity him from the bottom of my heart and point out to him that upon the banner of every religion will soon be written, in spite of resistance: "Help and not Fight", "Assimilation and not Destruction," "Harmony and Peace and not Dissension."[10] This idea, as it is found, is the core of neo-political philosophy that introduces a human outlook in politics in the international field.

Thus, Vivekananda evaluates the true significance of religion as 'Assimilation' that can be explained as the introduction of unity in men through the development of universal humanistic outlook on the basis of a principle of "Help and not Fight" which will lead us to the ultimate goal of human life and society: "Harmony and peace." This new synthetic and humanistic outlook of Swamiji's philosophy of religion may be taken as his philosophy of man which is evaluated by Marie Louisie Burke as "'*Darshan*' was unheard of in America, but here at the Parliament was a spontaneous and unconscious manifestation of the attraction of the human soul to the spiritually great."[11]

With this idea of spirituality in man as his greatness, Vivekananda worked in America and other parts of the world and delivered lectures for awakening humanity towards the completeness of Man in "Harmony and Peace." For introduction and development of this humanistic ideal Swamiji visited important cities of the East and the Middle West America such as Chicago, Iowa, St. Louis, Detroit, Boston, Baltimore, Cambridge. New York, Washington etc. After America he went to England and worked till the end of July, 1896. From London he went to France, Switzerland, Italy, Germany, Holland etc. During his visit, he came in contact with great men and women like Max Muller of the Oxford University, Miss Henrietta Muller, Miss Margaret E. Noble (Sister Nivedita), who were inspired by him and sacrificed their selves for the betterment of life and outlook of men. In the observation of Rabindranath Tagore, we may evaluate this humanistic programme of Vivekananda. Tagore points out, "Vivekananda's gospel marked the awakening of man in his fullness and that is why it inspired our youth to the diverse courses of liberation through work and sacrifice." This is the inner significance of his humanistic thought and activities which are for 'the awakening of man' through 'work and sacrifice.'

It should be mentioned in this connection that he visited different places of the world for incorporating this eternal and creative spirit of man into the Western civilisation through an expansion of the synthetic ideas of "Work and sacrifice" as expounded in *Upanishad* as *'Tena Tyaktena bhunjitha':* This synthetic programme expresses the secret of the material greatness that inspired the rich to supply him money for the collection of adequate funds for the welfare of the people and for the foundation of *Vedanta* Societies or centres so learning at many places of the world for expansion of intercultural and humanistic process. In this way Vivekananda worked for man for the synthetic development of humanistic outlook as the religion of life and existence which, in the observation of Vivekananda, is nothing but an inauguration of the highest consciousness in man as universal unity or harmony in human existence. In the observation of Romain Rolland, this humanistic programme of Vivekananda may be evaluated in the following way. He writes, "Moreover for a mind such as his, religion can never be fixed for ever in certain texts, under whatever form they may appear. It progressed. If it stopped for a single instant it died. His universal ideal was always in motion. It was to be fertilised, by the constant union of the East and the West, neither of them fixed in one doctrine or one point of time, but both living and advancing. And one of the objects of the Vedanta Society was to watch that a continual interchange of man and ideas took place, so that the circulation of the blood of thought should be regular and bathe the entire body of humanity."[12]

Cultivation of Practical and Synthetic Spirit of Humanity

With the humanistic process of expressing Unity in man and world in an intercultural relation of the East and the West as 'a continual interchange of men and ideas', Vivekananda prescribed certain principles of humanity as religion or philosophy of man and then introduced also some practical procedures for the application of those principles in life and society.

He reached Calcutta on 20th January, 1897. The people of Bengal and India accepted him with deep respect and paid their homage to this heroic son of Bengal. This inspired Swamiji to go through the institutional procedure for a practical purpose of establishing the ideal of *humanism* in the religious and the social life of men. Romain Rolland explained this institutional process of Vivekananda in the following ways. He wrote, "Vivekananda spoke as the master. He said that without strict organisation nothing lasting could be established. In a country like India it was not wise to begin such an organisation on the republican system, where in each had an equal voice and where decisions were according to the vote of a majority. It would be high time for that when the members had learnt to subordinate their interests and their particular prejudices to the public weal. What they wanted for the time being was a dictator. Moreover, he himself was only acting in the capacity of a servant of the common Master-In *nomineet in signo Ramakrishna-as* were they all."[13]

For the fulfillment of this purpose, an association was founded on 1st May, 1897, in the name of his great Master, which was known as the Ramakrishna Mission. The fundamental object of this mission is to awake the ideal of humanity, potent in man, that helps him to apply this outlook in his practical life: "This new Mission is to preach the truths which Sri Ramakrishna has, for the good of humanity, preached and demonstrated by practical application in his own life; and to help others to put these truths into practice in their lives for their temporal, mental and spiritual advancement…" The practical embodiment of the human outlook in the life of Sri Ramakrishna, towards the development of the idea of unity and eternity in all religions, urged Vivekananda to introduce the principle of unity, "for the establishment of fellowship among the followers of different religions, knowing them all to be only so many forms of one undying Eternal Religion." After the introduction of the general principles expressing the fundamental object of this institutions, there is an emphasis on practical methods.

As man lives in this material world, so it is the duty of a man to acquire the material fitness for ascertaining his existence in society. Material fitness of man produces mental fitness that helps him to go through the common principles of science, philosophy and religion, which finally leads to the unity and interrelation of men in the world. So "its methods of actions are (I) to train men so as to make them competent to teach such knowledge or sciences as are conducive to the material and spiritual welfare of the masses; (II) to promote and encourage arts and industries; (III) to introduce and spread among the people in general vedantic and other religious ideas as elucidated in the life of Ramakrishna."[14]

Though Swamiji started his life from his motherland and thought and worked for the betterment of the common life of Indians, still his final and fundamental end of life was to achieve the completeness of mankind in general on the basis of the establishment of the ideal of humanity through the development of interrelation of the East and the West. For this, he wanted to open different branches and centres of this Mission at different places of the world through which this human outlook of religion could be circulated, among men. For this Mission has two branches of action- (1) Indian work Department: Different Maths and Ashrmas were to be established at different parts of India "for the training of *Sannyasins* and such of the householders as may be willing to devote their lives to the teaching of others." (2) Foreign Department: Different trained members were to be sent to the countries outside India for the foundation of different centres "for the preaching of Vedanta in order to bring about a closer relation and better understanding between India and foreign countries."

Swamiji became the General President, Swami Brahmananda and Swami Yogananda were the President and the Vice-President of the Calcutta centre respectively and Sasi Maharaj (Swami Ramakrishnanandaji) went to Madras, Gangadhar Maharaj (Swami Akhandanandaji) went to Sargachi, Sarat Maharaj (Swami Saradanandaji) and Kali Maharaj (Swami Abhedanandaji) took the charge of America and London for the foundation of other centres at these places.

It should be noted in this connection that the supreme end of this Mission is to develop the potentiality of man as the manifestation of perfection or completeness that helps him to establish the relation of unity or interrelation among men beyond the different limitations and contradictions of life, created out of different finite and limited approaches to life through a self-centred process of narrow politics. For this, "The aims and ideals of the Mission being pure spiritual and humanitarian, it shall have no connection with politics".

This 'spiritual and humanitarian' outlook and activities of The Ramakrishna Mission as developed by Swami Vivekananda in different directions were evaluated by Romain Rolland in the following manner. He wrote, "The definitely social, humanitarian, and pan human apostolic nature of the order founded by Vivekananda is obvious. Instead of opposing, as do most religions, faith to reason and the stress and necessity of modem life, it was to take its place with science in the front rank; it was to co-operate with progress, material as well as spiritual, and to encourage arts and industries. But its real object was the good of the masses. It laid down that the essence of its faith was the establishment of brotherhood among the different religions, since their harmony constituted the Eternal Religion. The whole was under the aegis of Ramakrishna, whose great heart embraced all mankind within its love."[15] In the development of this humanistic programme in love, Vivekananda expanded the spirit of unity among men in this world. In this humanistic spirit and programme, Mahatma Gandhi observed the significance of the ideal and activities of Vivekananda. These inspired him to express, "I have gone through his works very thoroughly and after having gone through them the love that I had for my country became a thousand fold."[16] Like Gandhiji many people of India were stimulated by him and for the systematic form of stimulating men and expanding love and unity he accepted institutional process of the Ramakrishna Mission.

After the foundation of The Ramakrishna Mission, Swamiji again visited Almora, Amritsar, Srinagar, Rawalpindi, Lahore, Khetri, Jodhpur, Dehradun, Kashmir, Amarnath etc. and discussed before men the common features of the religion, philosophy and culture and this essential relation to human life and environment. After his visit to different places at different times, he came back to Calcutta on 18th October, 1890, and thought seriously about the foundation of an important centre for men, based on a strong foundation of the humanistic outlook of Sri Ramakrishna as a symbol of unity and on 9th December, 1898, The Ramakrishna Math was established at Belur, "which practised a grand harmony of all creeds and faiths as exemplified in the life of Sri Ramakrishna, and only idea of religion in its universal aspect would be preached. And from this centre of universal toleration would go forth the shining message of goodwill and peace and harmony to deluge the world."[17]

The shining message of goodwill and peace and harmony as Vivekananda's religion of humanity is circulated in the world through this centre with its other branches at other places of the world, Swamiji himself also tried to spread this human outlook among men through his visit to different places, and for the fulfillment of this purpose of expanding humanistic idea, he started again for England and America on 20th June, 1899. On 3rd August, 1900, he reached Paris and on 7th September, he delivered a lecture in the Congress of the History of Religions that inspired Dr Jagadish Chandra Bose, noted thinker and distinguished scientist of our country and other Western scientists and thinkers very much. After his visit to the different places of the West with observation of the activities of different centres of the Ramakrishna Mission at different places, he returned to Belur on 9th December, 1900 via Egypt, Constantinople, Vienna, Athens etc. From Belur, he reached the Advaita Ashram at Mayavati on 3rd January, 1901; and then went to visit some places of East Bengal and Assam and went to Kamakshya, Shillong, Dacca, Langalbundh, Chandranath, Deobhog etc. Then in January of 1902, he went to Buddha Gaya and in February, he lived in Benaras for a month, when he was trying to withdraw himself from the worldly activities and gradually was proceeding towards the end of his journey in this material world.

In this way at the end of his worldly journey, on Friday, the 4th of July, 1902, he finally entered into *Mahasamadhi* as entering into the transcendental spirit of Unity, beyond this life and world, through the experiential process of cultivating unity in men in this world.

Thus, if the different states of life and activities of Vivekananda are carefully examined, it is found that there is an evolutionary progress and systematic development of his humanistic outlook towards the advancement of his synthetic idea which explains the material and social nature and the spiritual form of existence of a man in a synthetic manner. It finally leads to the inauguration of the transcendent idea of Unity through different experiential forms of expressing unity in this life and world. This synthetic vision of Vivekananda inspires him to develop a new form of humanistic philosophy of man as the religion of Man that establishes man in religion and religion on man. This may be treated as the introduction of the humanistic outlook in religion, expanding a synthetic programme of founding unity or harmony in men, religions, cultures, or communities.

The introduction of this unity in man is the expression of his universal existence in and through the differences that is the realisation of universal human outlook through a harmonious process of life for unity: "Unity in variety in the plan of the Universe. We are all men, and yet we are all distinct from one another. Apart of humanity I am with you, and as Mr So-and-so I am different from you. As a man you are separate from the woman; as a human being you are-one with the women. As a man, you are separate from the animal, but as living beings, man, woman, animal and plant are all one; and as existence, you are one with the whole universe."[18] The realisation of this universality expresses the universal outlook of man as his religion or culture which cultivates the spirit of unity in and through the differences of religions or cultures. Finally it may be taken as the ultimate realisation of universal existence as God: "That universal existence is God, the ultimate unity in the universe. In Him we are all one."[19] The realisation of this oneness or universality is to be treated as the spirituality of man, expanding his divinity as unity in all men in different religions, cultures or communities. This, in the observation of Vivekananda, is the cultivation of the philosophy of Man, The Spiritual when the ideas of God in different religions or philosophies appear to the transcendent form of non-dual Absolute or Oneness in man, manifested through the experiential processes of his life and existence as different forms of unity or oneness.

The significance of this spirituality in man lies in the realisation and expression of God as Unity in differences which does not deny the existence of differences. It, on the other hand, is manifested through ·the diversities in different degrees which is a harmonious process of overcoming differences through the realisation of perfection in man as the expansion of universal unity in human life and society in different stages.

This may be treated as the background of developing Vivekananda's philosophy of Man, The Spiritual which may be evaluated as the unity in existence and values. The human existence in the spiritual programme of Vivekananda, stands for diversities or pluralities, expressing the diverse natures, characters and qualities in different religions, cultures and communities as limitations and restrictions of life and existence. But significance of man lies in transcending these limitations through the process of interrelation and intercommunication. It, in the observation of Vivekananda, is a process of reconciliation as spiritualisation in developing Man, the Infinite, harmonising the differences in existence as finiteness. This may be treated as the total development of man which is evaluated by Rabindranath Tagore, "Vivekananda's gospel marked the awakening of man in his fullness...."[20]

The essence of the spirit of 'the awakening of man' lies in the transcendence of limitation or finiteness with advancement of his infiniteness 'in his fullness' as the development of transcendent or absolute value of unity or universality in its different experiential forms as expression of human values in the expansion of the religion of humanity. So religion of man as the expression of human nature with the realisation of humanity as the introduction of harmony in material, social and spiritual existences of man.

In this process, Vivekananda used the term religion not in a restricted or limited sense, but he, on the other hand, applied it in a wider, practical and progressive form which explains the inner essence of *Dharma* or Hinduism as socio-cultural unity or integration.

This is a humanistic process for human freedom in expanding oneness in human existence. In the observation of Rybakov, it may be evaluated in the following way: "For the religion to be an effective instrument in the fight for the progress of the country and emancipation of the masses, he very firmly shifted the inner accents in Hinduism and broadened the scope of religion, associating it with the field of practical work, and not of abstract judgments: "Religion is not words and not theory...Its essence is not in listening and accepting. It is in being and becoming."[21]

In this context it may be pointed out that Vivekananda's idea of religion is not a restrictive analysis of man as "abstract judgments", but is an evaluation of natural man as religion of man in expanding the philosophy of man as Man, The Spiritual. Its meaning is the natural analysis of 'being' as material and social existence for freedom in material and social context as "emancipation of the masses." But its significance lies in the form of becoming that is an introduction of the transcendent value of unity in different experiential or social processes in expanding the potential infiniteness of man as Man, The Spiritual.

This synthetic programme of Vivekananda, expanding the philosophy of Man, The Spiritual explains the socio-economic and spiritual nature and existence of man in an expansion of freedom in unity. This is evaluated by Bhupendra Nath Dutta, a socialist, in the following manner. He writes, "Swamiji was not Marxist, nor an economist. But he, in his foresight, has placed a programme before the countrymen, for introducing in India a society and new culture free from classes and castes. This new India will be able to develop union of the East and the West. Thus, the total meditation and dream of Swamiji will be fulfilled."[22]

In this analysis, we may observe the fundamental object of Vivekananda's philosophy of man in cultivating the synthetic spirit in his ideas of religion, philosophy and culture as an expansion of the synthetic ideal of Man, The Spiritual. This may be treated as natural and unconditional process of developing unity in natural existence of man as material, social and spiritual reconciliation. It is an experiential process of expanding unity in society in an intercultural and international context. This, in the background of developing the transcendent or spiritual value of unity, manifests the infinite potency of man as the expression of divinity and humanity in human existence in a socio-cultural form. In the words of Radhakrishnan, the inner spirit of this synthetic philosophy of man, can be evaluated thus: "He inculcated a religion of patriotism-not patriotism in the narrow sense of the word, but patriotism as the religion of humanity. His was a religion which called us to look upon all human beings as kindred, as belonging to one family. That is the kind of religion which he taught. us and which he adopted. He said "it is man making religion." It is humanistic religion. There is no divorce between contemplative life and social service. The two things are expressions of one and the same kind of phenomenon. If we have reached the supreme and felt the reality of God in our own minds and thoughts it would be our duty to come to the rescue of all people who are suffering in this world."[23] In this 'man-making' process we find the unity in existence as material or social and spiritual states of unity and unity in values as unity of ideals of humanity and divinity which may be treated as unity of transcendent or spiritual and experiential or socio-cultural processes as "contemplative life and social service" in expanding human freedom in unity in this world.

This synthetic spirit and programme as developed through life, thoughts and activities of Swami Vivekananda, cultivating his philosophy of Man, The Spiritual is accepted by Jawaharlal Nehru as 'great unifying force.' It expresses the creative essence of the philosophy of unity in pluralities as also manifested through the philosophy of life of other great Indian thinkers and social reformers like Sri Ramakrishna and Mahatma Gandhi. So the importance of life and activities of these great men, advancing a synthetic programme for developing harmony in human existence in this world, is finally evaluated by Nehru in the following way; "Men like Sri Ramakrishna Paramahansa, men like Swami Vivekananda and men like Mahatma Gandhi are great unifying forces, great constructive geniuses of the world not only in regard to the particular teachings that they taught, but their approach to the world and their conscious and unconscious influence on it is of most vital importance to us..."[24]

In this way life and activities of Swami Vivekananda are observed as closely associated with his philosophy of Man, The Spiritual which may be treated as the religion of Man as the natural expression of human nature, unfolding the creative infiniteness in man in expanding intercultural unity in worldly existence.

Notes and References

1. *Swami Vivekananda Centenary Memorial Volume,* 1963, p. 335.
2. Nivedita, S., *The Master as I Saw Him,* 1948, p. 230.
3. S. N. Dhar, *A Comparative Biography of Swami Vivakananda;* 1975, pp. 398-400.
4. *Sri Aurobindo,* Vol. II, 1971, p. 171.

5. Response to Welcome Address at the Parliament of Religions, Chicago, 11th September, 1893, *Complete Works of Swami Vivekananda,* Birth Cent. Edition, 1963, Vol. I, p. 4.
6. Paper on Hinduism, read at the Parliament of Religions on 19th September, 1893, *Complete Works of Swami Vivekananda.,* Birth Cent, Edition, 1963, Vol. I. p. 14.
7. *Ibid.,* p. 17.
8. *Ibid.,* p. 17.
9. *Ibid.,* p. 19.
10. *Ibid.,* p. 24.
11. Marie Louise Burke, *Swami Vivekananda in America:* New Discoveries, 1958, p. 67.
12. Rolland, R., *The Life of Vivekananda and the Universal Gospel;* 1979, Vol. II, pp. 83-84.
13. *Ibid.,* pp. 119-120.
14. *Ibid.,* p. 120.
15. *Ibid.,* p. 121.
16. *Prabuddha Bharat,* May, 1963, p. 170.
17. *Life of Swami Vivekananda,* Vol. II, 2nd Edition, Mayavati, p. 735.
18. The idea of a Universal Religion, *Complete Works of Swami Vivekananda,* Birth Cent. Edn., 1963, VII. II, p. 381.
19. *Ibid,* p. 381.
20. *World Thinkers on Ramakrishna- Vivekananda,* 1983, p. 35.
21. R. B. Rybakov, *Bourgeois Reformation of Hinduism,* Swami Vivekananda Studies in Soviet Union,1987, p. 396.
22. Bhupendranath Dutta, *Swami Vivekananda,* 1393 B. S., p. 240.
23. S. Radhakrishnan, *Foreword, Swami Vivekananda Centenary Memorial Volume,* 1963, p. x.
24. *World Thinkers on Ramakrishna- Vivekananda,*1993, p. 45.

Chapter – 2

The Philosophical Significance of Man, The Spiritual: An Intercultural Development of the Religion of Humanity

Part – I

Religious, Scientific and Philosophical Prospects of Man

The synthetic outlook of Vivekananda, as developed through his life and activities, establishes a new form of religion which includes the nature and existence of man. Because religion, according to him, is nothing but the expression of human nature that is manifested completely through the expression of perfection in life and society. For the attainment of this perfection, Vivekananda propounds a synthetic view of religion above all contradictions, differences and dogmas, as religion, he observes, is a unifying agency that stands on the unity in life and society.

In the context of this analysis of the synthetic view of religion by Swami Vivekananda, we may refer to the fact that the old, narrow and conservative outlook of religion, devoid of scientific development of human life, creates much contradictions against the wider view of morality and welfare of the people. In the observations of MacIver and Page, it may be said that, "The more conservative religions have resisted the fresh moral insights and the social applications derive from advancing science."[1]

But with the development of social outlook as related to the advancement of science and religion in modern age, is coming very much close to humanity and thus also developing socio-moral and human relation of unity, which, in the opinion of MacIver and Page, "Religion, growing world-conscious, may well sustain the nearer sense of our community with one another and thus fall into consistency with a purely moral code."[2]

In the background of this synthetic observations, both science and religion are becoming more important and unique through their comprehensive approaches to the total development of humanity. In this line we, at present, are trying to find out the proper welfare and the real truth of man, that, we observe, stands on the unity of science and religion. It is because of that the progress in science makes the truth, as derived by religion, more definite; and the religion of humanity, on the other hand, makes the human welfare, as done by science, more significant.

This comprehensive development of man, done by science and religion, reveals the inner essence of Indian tradition or culture which is evaluated by Swami Ranganathananda thus: "...pure science, with its passion for truth and human welfare, will always remain as one of the noblest pursuits of man; and our country, which has nurtured this love and pursuit of truth in the fields of physical science, religion and philosophy in the past, must continue to nurture it in all fields in the modern age. Religion and philosophy in India, as given to us in our *Upanishadic* tradition, is but the continuation of the scientific search for truth at the sense-data level to the higher aesthetic, ethical and spiritual levels of experience...."[3]

Swami Vivekananda, with this rich Indian tradition and experience, explains rationally the relation of religion with science in the background of the idea of perfection as the unity of men in the world.

This view of Swamiji expresses a scientific outlook of religion that brings religion nearer to science, as both science and religion explain the human existence clearly and work for the welfare of the people. In this connection it may be said that as religion like all other social sciences, applies different methods for the analysis of human mind, Vivekananda observes, "All science has its particular methods; so has the science of religion. It has more methods also, because it has more material to work upon. The human mind is not homogeneous like the external world. According to the different natures, must there be different methods."[4] Through these different methods, sciences try to induce truths which are applicable to the physical world and religion also tries to induce truths about the reality of man and world. "Religion deals with the truths of the metaphysical world just as chemistry and the other natural sciences deal with the truths of the physical world."[5] Thus, different elements of truth, deduced by different sciences, can be applied on society for the betterment of the material life of man which are also to be re-established by the science of religion for the development of human nature towards unity, potential in man: "Yet through all minds runs a unity, and there is a science which may be applied to all. This science of religion is based on the analysis of the human soul. It has no creed."[6] So the science of religion that discovers unity in human soul, also produces unity in science and religion, as truths induced by sciences, establish the human outlook of religion on a strong foundation and the science of religion on the other hand makes the truth of science more creative and vital, through its application in human life towards unity. For this Radhakrishnan points out, "The need for religion, for a system of thought, for devotion to a cause which will give our fragile and fugitive existence significance and value does not require much elaborate argument. It is an intrinsic element of human nature."[7]

This new outlook of religion on the basis of the explanation and evaluation of the intrinsic nature of man as unity, is developed through a long course of evolution of religion and science emphasised the *Determinism,* because this world was taken as the mechanical evolution of the static conception of Matter; so human life according to these sciences was nothing but the change of physical and chemical processes and thus living organism was taken as the complex physico-chemical machine. This view of life and world established the philosophy of Materialism that explains the existence of man at the background of matter and so denies the existence of religion, as it, according to this view, is unreal and imaginary. Carvakas, the Indian Materialists, also deny religion, as it has no necessity in the explanation of human life and world. This idea of Materialism thus explains the nature of religion in a negative sense that paves the way for the development of the negative outlook of religion as advanced by *Positivism, Naturalism and Agnosticism.*

But this negative view of religion is to be changed through the introduction of the modern outlook of science, when it changes the old idea of matter as dead and inactive. Modern physicists like Planck, Rutherford, Bohr, Millikan, discovered the electrical nature of atom, that introduced *Dynamism* in the idea, of matter, and it changed the traditional static view of matter. In the beginning of this century Einstein propounded the *Theory of Relativity* which made a radical change in the classical view of matter and energy which were regarded as separate entities of nature. Matter can he converted into energy (Nuclear Fusion) and energy can be converted in matter (Pair production). The old *dualism* between matter and motion was vanished and finally both were identified. This identity of matter and energy thus introduces a change in the idea of dead matter, that, according to Eddington and James Jeans, also brought the material explanations nearer to life and mind. This is not inconsistent with the idealistic interpretation or religious explanation of human life and world. The development of this new outlook inspires Lord Balfour to express, "we know too much about matter to be any longer materialists."

Here we are trying to say that the fundamental character of matter as studied by the ancient scientists was of matter (atom) an idea, totally opposed to the notion of the spirit which is pervasively present. The present discoveries in the atom of a continuity and pervasiveness, brings it closer to the notion suggested by the spirit of religious consciousness. So with the development of scientific consciousness, the scientific explanation of matter comes closer to religions or spiritual consciousness.

Now it is also a time for the upholders of religious experience to declare that religious consciousness as indicated in the spirit is non-different from the advanced notion of matter (atom) by the present scientists-hence the gulf between the two orders of experiences, science and religion has been closed up, only they remain distinct as two different approaches and their procedures and pursuits are different or will remain different.

In this way the dynamic change in material science thus changes the materialistic view of life and introduces a new idea in life science, when life is: taken as a Vital Force because the sign of life in a smallest protoplasm proves that life does not come from a mere material composition. John Caird writes, "The protoplasm which can be analysed and of which the chemical constitution is known, is not living but dead protoplasm, whilst that protoplasm which can be designated living though containing similar elements with that which is not living, manifests qualities or functions that are totally new, and of which, therefore, cannot be ascribed to its merely chemical or physical composition."[8] This new phenomenon in living organism is called life which is not derived from non-living matter. Life, on the other hand, is a superior power that controls all material activities that leads to a teleological development of the idea of unity in practice and in the activities of a complex living organism like man. Thus, Caird explains, "Here we come upon the conception of unity of which the idea or end is not arbitrarily imposed from without,...on certain independent materials, but it is the result of an internal spontaneity or self-activity, working out diversities of member, form, function, from its own inherent self-producing energy and at the same time, in the very act of differentiating, reintegrating its diversities into the common unity. Here, also, instead of the end being outward and accidental to the means, it is their own immanent end, instead of the parts being used up for the production of the end, we have membered totality in the production and maintenance of which the parts have their own natural fulfillment or realisation."[9]

This new scientific outlook as the introduction of unity in the development of living organism, throws a new light on the explanation of the nature and existence of man and establishes an intimate relation between science and religion. Religion explains the essence or reality of man and different sciences deal with its various expressions and appearances in the material world. In this way the truth in man as discovered by religion, is examined by sciences in and through the practical human life that finally inspires religion to introduce universal, wider, free and practical principle in human life and world. This development of scientific outlook, thus, urges religion to be free from old dogmas, contradictions through the introduction of unity and universality in human life; and science, on the other hand, through a contact with this universality as discovered by religion, tries to cross its limitations of observations and experiments and enters into a synthetic view about life, that makes it nearer to religion. For this Bacon points out, "A little science makes man atheist, whereas a great deal of science turns the man's thought to religion." Admitting the above statements of science and religion, one has to distinguish them as two distinct approaches to determine experience, but they reach a common result. These past oppositions no longer remain or persist. Thus, this close relation of science and religion makes them more intimate towards the explanation of a common objective in human life and world. Eddington rightly observes, "You will understand the true spirit neither of science nor of religion unless seeking is placed in the forefront."[10] In this context it may be pointed out that the material explanation of science acquires its significance through the inauguration of a general and common purpose behind both sciences and religions that urges to explain the evolution of the world and man towards a common goal which is to be cultivated in the line of their mutual advanced aspects. This is a positivistic programme of explaining the total nature of the universe that is a process of evaluating the internal and the external aspects of being, explored as mind and matter. In this background modern science examines both these aspects of being for explaining the total and coherent nature of the world. For this it may be said thus: "The true physics is that which will, one day, achieve the inclusion of man in his wholeness in a coherent picture of the world."[11] The significance of this idea of "a coherent picture of the world," lies in the explanation of unity in idea and existence as the totality of being, exhibiting the wholeness of man in the world. This develops the scientific outlook of religion and establishes a broader idea of religion for man which finally is to be evaluated as the religion of Man.

The Religion of Man as the Realisation of Man, The Spiritual

The common objective about the man and the world discovered through the developed process of science and religion inspired Vivekananda to avoid the traditional dogmatic outlook of religion and science. Religion, in his opinion, is the way of the life of a man to become the Man in its true spirit or outlook as Vivekananda points out, "Religion is neither word nor doctrine. It is to be and become, not to hear and accept. It is whole soul changed into that which it believes." It is a broad and liberal attitude towards life as a whole viewing all other aspects as to be lifted to a higher prospect with a sense of values.

Thus, in this process of becoming the Man, which is a process of progressive transformation, an individual gradually realises the significance of his highest existence within him, which, according to Vivekananda, is the realisation of the Truth. Religion is thus, to be taken as this realisation of the supreme value of man. So the primary meaning of religion, according to Vivekananda, should be the realisation of Man in its innermost core, that is the manifestation of perfection as Truth or God: "The greatest name man ever gave to God is Truth. Truth is the fruit of realisation; therefore seek it within the soul."[12] In this way the realisation of the deeper core of Man within this material body of the individual urges him to ignore the limitations and contradictions caused by this material body and thus also inspires him to transcend the limitations of nature or material contradictions of this material world by a transformation: "Freedom, O Freedom; Freedom, O Freedom; is the song of the soul. Bondage, alas, to be bound in nature, seems its fate."[13] So the realisation of Truth or the highest existence of man as Man, expresses the fundamental meaning of religion that finally inspires man to become free from the nature or the. contradictions of the world where he is born and reaches his highest state of life where he himself becomes the 'Master of nature': "Man says to himself, 'I am born slave, I am bound; nevertheless, there is a Being who is not bound by nature. He is free and Master of nature."[14] This is the creative potentiality in man, that, through its development towards its highest manifestation; makes a man a Master over nature or material world where he is created. The expression of this religion of man is according to science, the expression of the greatest mystery of Man. Mr Lincolm Barnett rightly observes, "For man is enchained by the very condition of his being, his fitness and involvement in nature. The further he extends his horizons, the more vividly he recognises the fact that, as the physicist Niels Bohr puts it, 'we are both spectators and actors in the great drama of existence.' Man is thus his own greatest mystery."[15]

This advanced and changed scientific outlook about the mystery of Man as created and creative entity, inspires Vivekananda to explain the end of his religion as the religion of man or the proper expression of the nature of man in this world. In the explanation of human nature in its spiritual transformation from basic Nature to Man led Swamiji not to ignore the material existence of the individual in this material world; but to regard it as its basis, inspiring him towards a spiritual process, which is a freedom from the material order or other subsequent orders of Nature-chemical or biological. It is a cry of freedom by a transforming process, so that Vivekananda could say: "Bondage and liberty, light and shadow, good and evil must be there, but the very fact of the bondage shows also this freedom hidden there. If one is fact, the other is equally a fact."[16]

The reality of this fact proves the significance of the existence of man towards becoming Man through a process of evolution, where man starts through his existence in this world which becomes perfect through a gradual manifestation of his perfect nature, potential in him. In this process, Rabindranath Tagore also observes, "The larger co-operative units could adequately pay for a greater freedom of self-expression, and they began to form and develop in their bodies new organs of power, new instruments of efficiency. This was the march of evolution ever unfolding the potentialities of life."[17]

So this gradual unfolding of human nature proves the uniqueness of human mind in the human body where he tries to realise his existence as Man in the highest form of human freedom. It is a process towards a transformation, which is attitudinal. In *Evolution After Darwin,* (Vol. III), Sir Julian Huxley evaluates this process thus: "Man's evolution is not biological but psychological; it operates by the mechanism of cultural tradition, which involves the cumulative self-reproduction and self-variation of mental activities and their products." In this context of analysis it may be noted that the evolution of man is the mental development of man towards the realisation of the highest perfection in him, when he tries to rise above the external contradictions in the material world and internal contradiction due to materialist attitudes of mind. This way of developing man is explained by Vivekananda, "Man is man so long as he is struggling to rise above nature, and this nature is both internal and external."[18]

In this process of the development of man, Vivekananda finds the necessity of religion that explains the significance of man's evolution. Regarding this explanations, Vivekananda points out, "Two theorics have gained some acceptance amongst modern scholars. One is the spirit theory of religion, the other the evolution of the idea of the Infinite. One party maintains that ancestor worship is the beginning of religious ideas, the other, that religion originates in the personification of the powers of nature."[19] Swamiji tries to reconcile these two extreme explanations about man, when he says, "These two views, though seem to be contradictory, can be reconciled on a third basis, which to my mind is the real germ of religion, and that I propose to call the struggle to transcend the limitations of the senses."[20] Thus, through this process of transcending the limitations, a man tries to overcome his finiteness and gradually realises his infinite existence in him: "So man has to give up the plane of matter and rise to other spheres to seek a deeper expression of that Infinite."[21]

In the expression of Infinite in the finite man, Vivekananda observes the real significance of the evolution of man as the development of inner life of man through a gradual manifestation of infinite power in him. He points out, "...that man can not be simply an evolution. Every evolution presupposes an involution. The modern scientific man will tell you that you can only get the amount of energy out of a machine which you have previously put into it. Something cannot be produced out of nothing. If a man is an evolution of the molluse, then the perfect man - the Buddha-man, the Christ-man was involved in the molluse. If it is not so, whence come these gigantic personalities? Something cannot come out of nothing."[22]

In this connection it may be said that Vivekananda, in the light of modern science, observes that life is not a mere expression of matter, but on the other hand he explains the importance of the existence of the human life as something beyond the limitation of his material finiteness. Swamiji points out, "Thus, we are in the position of reconciling the scriptures with modern light. That energy which manifests itself slowly through various stages until it becomes the perfect man cannot come out of nothing. It existed somewhere; and if the molluse or the protoplasm is the first point to which you can trace it, that protoplasm, somehow or other, must have contained the energy."[23]

The energy is the Spirit, which is a continuous urge, as involved process towards a lift. Thus, the advanced scientific outlook of Swamiji, tries to set aside the old controversy about the material and spiritual views of man; and introduces his prospective religious outlook that tries to explain the spiritual basis of human existence in the milieu of other processes of Nature from matter. He writes, "There is a great discussion going on as to whether the aggregate of materials we call the body is the cause of manifestation of the force we call the soul, thought etc. or whether it is the thought that manifests this body. The religions of the world of course hold that the force called thought, manifests the body, and not the reverse."[24] The thought as referred to here, is lifting-process of the energy-continuum from Matter to Man.

The religious explanation, according to Vivekananda, supplies the true significance of human existence as it does not take man as the mere expression of matter, but religion holds that the material existence of human being becomes perfect through the development of Man's inner spirit in him. So Vivekananda thinks that this transformed idea of man explains the place of true religion or real nature of man, as he writes, "The body is not the Real Man, neither is the mind, for the mind waxes and wanes. It is the spirit beyond, which alone can live forever."[25] The spirit gives continuity to human aspirations, by transforming Man. Thus, through this development of the inner spirit, the transforming element, an eternal or infinite spirit of Man, comes out from the finiteness of the individual when the finite man realises the significance of its infinity in him. Rabindranath, like Vivekananda, also observed this evolution of the true nature of man through the development of his inner infinite spirit. In *Manuser Dharma,* he writes, "In the vast evolution of the world we come across the first meaning in life particles, then in animals and finally in man. The outer doors begin to open one after the other, till we come to the innermost region of man. Here we find the finite soaked in the infinite." The infinity chases the finitude of Man and man is lifted to a highest process.

Thus, we may hold that the development of the infiniteness in man is the real expression of the significance of human existence through which an individual acquires his perfect individuality. This, according to Vivekananda, is the proper meaning of the religion of man as the expression of the real nature of man as Infinite: "We are struggling towards individuality, and that is the Infinite, that is the real nature of man."[26] It is a rise to an integral consciousness and attitude - a transformed and evolved position of Man in Expansion.

In this way, by explaining the nature of man as Infinite, above all his finite contradictions, Vivekananda tries to explain the potential nature of man as Infinite Man which, according to him, is his proper religion that finally explains the process of human life of becoming Man, The Spiritual as expressing the religiosity of his Nature.

The Humanistic Emergence of Divinity as Spirituality

After the explanation of the meaning of the religion of man as the evolution of the real nature of man towards the development of his highest existence as Infinite, Vivekananda evaluated the proper significance of this meaning of religion as the realisation of divinity in man as his proper spirituality which is the manifestation of infinity in the finite existence of the individual. This is a development of consciousness, by one's sincere effort and self-dedication into this super process towards the realisation of one's perfection in life.

Though the individual existence of man is finite, limited and material, still the real understanding of his existence as Man does not lie in his finiteness, it exists in the realisation of 'Infinite I' in him. This, according to Vivekananda, is the self-realisation of man through a concrete evaluation of his divine nature behind apparent material existence in the world by an effort and activity. Man, according to Vivekananda, exists in physical, mental and spiritual orders, but his individuality lies in acquiring of perfect freedom from the basic orders of pursuing towards unrestricted processes and attitudes towards 'Infinite Self' beyond all the finite restrictedness: "Vivekananda proceeded to analyse the physical, mental and soul attributes of life. The body is but a shell; the mind something that acts but a brief and fantastic part; while the soul has distinct individuality in itself.

To realise the infinity of self is to attain "freedom" which is the Hindoo word for "Salvation."[27]

The *Upanishads* refer to two souls in man, the lower and the higher or real soul: The lower self 'ego' is expressed through the material existence in this world, and the real self is *Atman* or pure and infinite being of man. The *Upanishad* compares these two existences of self with two birds sitting on the branch of a tree; one enjoys the fruits and the other exists as the pure witness or silent being.

Following *Upanishads* Vivekananda also explains the two stages of human life, one is the expression of material existence as lower self and the other transcends this lower stage of life through the expression of the higher order of existence of Man as pure being or the spirit through the expression of his divinity or perfection in him that leads to the realisation of unrestricted experience: "Every individual has in himself perfection. It lies within the dark recesses of his physical being. To say that a man has become good because God gave him a portion of His perfection is to conceive the Divine Being as God minus just so much perfection as he has imparted to a person on this earth. The inexorable law of science proves that the soul is individual and must have perfection within itself, the attainment of which means freedom, not salvation,...and the realisation of "individual infinity...Nature! God! Religion! It is all one."[28]

So, the specialty of man, according to Vivekananda, is not to be found in man's confinement to the lower order of human life as 'ego', but it is the inauguration of Unity or Oneness in man as the invocation of his integrality or infinity in him through which he realised his non-duality between himself and reality as a whole: "I am Existence Absolute, Bliss Absolute; Knowledge Absolute, I am He."[29]

This realisation of non-duality with he whole universe, according to Swamiji, is the realisation of *Atman* or Soul, beyond all limitations and changes of body and mind ...This highest state of life and consciousness can transcend all limitation and contradiction through the development of unity in all, which is formless and infinite being as it is one and exists in all individuals. The realisation of this highest state of life as one and Infinite Being, is the manifestation of the highest existence as God. This procedure towards the development of the higher stage of life, as Vivekananda observes, proves the real significance of the evolution of the real nature of man, where he gradually tries to realise his perfection in him through the renunciation of all imperfections or finiteness of life. Vivekananda explains: "... the proof of evolution is simply this: You find a series of bodies from the lowest to the highest rising in a gradually ascending scale...our struggle for the higher life shows that we have been degraded from a high state. It must be so, only it may vary as to details. I always cling to the idea set forth with one voice by Christ, Buddha, and the *Vedanta*, that we must all come to perfection in time, but only by giving up this imperfection...we must go to the Reality. Renunciation will take us to it."[30]

So, renunciation is the transcendence of the limitations and evils of life as 'separate self' or 'ego', that urges man to develop a real goodness in him through which he realises his perfect nature as God, which according to Swamiji is a 'joyful state of existence.' Thus, Vivekananda writes, "Renunciation is the very basis of our true life; every moment of goodness and real life that we enjoy is when we do not think of ourselves. This little separate self must die. Then we shall find that we are in the Real, and that Reality is God, and He is our true nature, and He is always in us and with us. Let us live in Him and stand in Him. It is the only joyful state of existence. Life on the plane of the spirit is the only life, and let us all try to attain to this realisation."[31]

The realisation of this 'joyful state' is the understanding of the *Brahman* as the highest human value as Absolute Bliss or Joy which is manifested in human life in different degrees through the process of renunciation or the negation of ignorance. Swamiji points out, "Every moment really we are enjoying the absolute bliss, though covered up, misunderstood, and caricatured. Wherever there is any blessing, blissfulness, or joy, even the joy of the thief in stealing, it is that absolute bliss coming out, only it has become obscured, muddled up, as it were, with all sorts of extraneous conditions, and misunder stood. But to understand that, we have to go through the negation, and then the positive side will begin. We have to give up ignorance and all that is false, and then truth will begin to reveal itself to us. When we have grasped the truth, things which we gave up at first will take new shape and form, will appear to us in a new light, and become deified."[32]

Overcoming Contradictions as Maya or Avidya

The inauguration of this idea of truth in a new form, thus rejects the unreality or untruth as *maya* or *avidya* as ignorance about the true nature of reality in man. It proves the contradictions in human life as they exist in life and existence in this material world, expressing the contradictory nature of reality or truth. So *maya* or *avidya,* according to Vivekananda, is nothing but the experience of contradictions as it shows the empirical reality of the good and evil that one confronts in life and world at the same time. Swamiji writes, "Thus, we find that *maya* is not a theory for the explanation of the world: it is simply a statement of facts as they exist, that the very basis of our being is contradiction, that everywhere we have to move through this tremendous contradiction, that wherever there is good, there must also be evil, and wherever there is evil, there must be some good, wherever there is life, death must follow as its shadow, and everyone who smiles will have to weep, and vice-versa."[33]

In this connection it may be said that the significance of this explanation of the nature of *maya* lies not in the rejection of the reality of human life and world but in the rejection of contradictions in man and world due to *maya* or *avidya* which can be possible through the introduction of the idea of Absolute Reality as unity in diversities or contradictions as it is manifested in human life and world in different forms in different degrees. This is a world of good and evil. Wherever there is good, evil follows, but beyond and behind all these manifestations, all these contradictions, the *Vedanta* finds out that Unity. It says, "Give up what is evil and give up what is good." What remains then? Behind good and evil stands something which is yours, the real you, beyond every evil, and beyond every good too, and it is that which is manifesting itself as good and bad."[34] Vivekananda, thus in the light of *Advaita Vedanta*, explains the manifestation of this Absolute Existence in and through the existence of life and in this world: "Here is the Absolute (a) and this the universe, (b) The Absolute has become the universe. By this is not only meant the material world, but the mental world, the spiritual world-heavens and earths, and in fact, everything that exists."[35] So it is to be noted here, that Vivekananda does not deny the reality of man and world, but on the other he accepts them as the real manifestation of Absolute which is fundamentally existent: "This world is the evolution of nature and the manifestation of God. It is our interpretation of *Brahman* or the Absolute, seen through the veil of *Maya* or appearance. The world is not zero, it has a certain reality; it only appears because *Brahman* is."[36]

In the introduction of the idea of the Absolute as manifested in and through the human life and the world, Vivekananda, like Hegel, the Western Absolutist, firstly accepts this life and world as the expression of Absolute; where finites are to be taken as the finite manifestations of the Infinite and thus all contradictions in the finite life and world are to be reconciled through the expression of this infinite idea as unity.

Secondly, Vivekananda, like Hegel, also accepts contradictions in the process of life and world. But Absolute is an idea of completeness that includes contradictions also. So Absolute as introduced by Vivekananda in his religion of man, is due to the presentation of the idea of completeness or harmony of or the reconciliation of contradictions in the finite life and world.*

So in this connection it may further be said, that the contradictions and limitations are to be reconciled in human life through the development of his highest existence as Infinite consciousness. Thus, in Hegel's philosophy we find that the Absolute consciousness includes the logico-dialectical process which is manifested in human life and human reason or consciousness also, proceeding harmoniously towards the development of Divine Reason or

---

* Rabindranath also abserves, "At the dawn of religious consciousness we realise that the harmony of the whole lies in accepting and transcending the contradictions of opposites. —"Amar Dharma" in Atmaparichay.

Consciousness in him. Rabindranath also writes, "the external nature and my reason are the expression of the same reason."[37] Again Vivekananda, "in this context, represents the *Vedantic* view of Absolute, who is *Saccidananda,* and where existence is consciousness as Bliss that is nothing but pure and Infinite, Being or Existence. The human being tries to realise this Infiniteness more and more in different stages of life, beyond his finiteness. But the total nature of idea of this Absolute value can not be fully exhausted in any limited stage of human life, so man's realisation of Absolute is taken as partial and limited and this idea is explained as something, beyond this limitation. Vivekananda tries to evaluate the nature of this infinite idea, "We sometimes indicate a thing by describing its surroundings. When we say, *'Sat-Chit-Ananda'* (Existence-Knowledge-Bliss) we are merely indicating the shores of an indescribable Beyond. Nor can we say, is' about it, for that too is relative. Any imagination, any concept is in vain, *neti, neti* ('not this, not this') is all that can be said, for even to think is to limit and so to loose."[38]

In the context of this analysis of Vivekananda, it may be pointed out that he has not denied the existence of man and world as unreal, on the other hand he has accepted their relative reality in the background of the ultimate state of unity as *Brahman.* Modern researches in Physics are also urging to oneness or an ultimate state of unity. Einstein in his life was absorbed in the 'Unified Field Theory' with a view to establishing the fact that one single force among the four basic forces must control the diverse phenomena of the universe both in the macroscopic and in the microscopic fields. These basic forces are gravitation, electromagnetic forces, strong and weak interaction nuclear forces. Einstein did not, however, succeed in attaining the goal. But latter researches in this field revealed unified electromagnetic and weak interaction forces on which Professor A. Salam and others worked and were awarded Nobel Prize. Also in the field of elementary particles (Bosons and Fermions), that build up matter and energy, and act as intermediaries of the above mentioned basic forces. Particle physicists are of firm conviction that a single particle 'euark' could be the basic one. The combinations of different forms of which (up-down, charm-strange, top-bottom) form the entire world of elementary particles and their antiparticles.

In this context of the analysis of the state of unity, we may also place the observation of V.S. Kostychenko. Regarding the development of the state he writes, "...it is said that it corresponds most satisfactorily to the urge of science for unity: the ideal of chemistry is to reduce all elements to one 'basic element', the ideal of physics is to reduce all forms of energy to one 'basic energy', and in *Brahman* is precisely achieved this maximum unity, and the absolute homogeneous beginning of all existence turns out to have been found."[39] So, in the context of absolute knowledge of unity as the highest state as *Brahman,* different states of worldly existence are coherent and thus Mr Kostyuchenko observes "...in scientific knowledge in general, and in scientific experience in particular, the differentiation between the direct and the indirect is always relative, conventional, mobile."[40]

In the background of this scientific evaluation, it may be noted that the real significance of Vivekananda's spiritual outlook is to accept all the material, social and spiritual states of human existence in the world and to explain all these states as 'relative,' 'conventional,' and 'mobile'. As all these states are coherently related to each other, so these are 'relative' and 'conventional' and as different states of existence manifest the particular aspects of reality and coherently proceed towards the development of the absolute nature of Reality as Absolute or *Brahman*, so these are 'mobile' or dynamic.

Unity of Man and God

Thus, Vivekananda, in the light of the traditional or conventional outlook of *Vedanta*, and the mobile or dynamic spirit of modern culture, explains two aspects of reality as the phenomenal and the transcendental and thus becomes transcendentalist and spiritualist. The manifestation of Absolute in this life and world represents the phenomenal character of reality which is expressed in and through the differences and contradictions of this material world and so may be changeable in nature. As it appears in this world in different forms in different manners, this can be recognised as the personal God or *Ishvara,* who is immanent in this world and is personally related to the finite life and the finite world.

But as this finiteness is the expression of Infiniteness, so infinite nature of Reality is to be realised more and more as pure form, who is to be taken as *Saccidananda* or pure Existence, Consciousness and Bliss. He is transcendent, because His Absolute nature cannot be fully exhausted in the limited and finite procedure of the human life and world. But this procedure towards Infiniteness, urges man to realise his infinite being in him, that gradually leads to the development of the highest state of life when there would be an inauguration of the feeling of non-duality. Vivekananda explains, "personal God is as much an entity for himself as we are for ourselves, and no more. As men we must need God, as gods we need none. This is why Sri Ramakrishna constantly saw the Divine Mother ever present with him, more real than anything around him; but in Samadhi all went but self. Personal God comes nearer and nearer until He melts away and there is no personal God and no more "I", all is merged in the Self."[41]

This is the infinite existence on the real essence of man, when he realises the Absolute value as *Saccidananda* like an infinite human being. Finite man, without the knowledge of his real infinite nature, suffers from the finiteness or contradictions in this material world, but a gradual realisation of the infiniteness in him finally leads to the highest accomplishment of the formless, pure, immutable, universal being of unity in him. Thus, in this process of the development of the highest state, there it is found, that the idea of personal god is merged into the impersonal oneness or Absolute, and, similarly, through the development of infinite existence of man there would be the final manifestation of Universal Man in finite human being. Swamiji evaluates this highest existence in a rational manner: "The idea grows and grows, until it attains its climax. In almost all of the Upanishads, we find the climax coming at the last, and that is the dethroning of this God of the universe. The personality of God vanishes, the impersonality comes. God is no more a person, no more a human being, however magnified and exaggerated, who rules the universe, but He has become 'an embodied principle in every being, immanent in the whole universe.' It would be illogical to go from the Personal God to the Impersonal, and at the same time to leave man as a person. So the personal man is broken down, and man as principle is built up. The person is only a phenomenon, the principle is behind it. Thus, from both sides, simultaneously, we find the breaking down of personalities and the approach towards principles, the Personal God approaching the Impersonal, the personal man approaching the Impersonal Man. Then come the succeeding stages of the gradual convergence of the two advancing lines of the Impersonal God and the Impersonal Man. And the *Upanishads* embody the stages through which these two lines at last become one, and the last word of each *Upanishad* is, 'Thou art That.' There is but One Eternally Blissful Principle, and that one is manifesting itself as all this variety."[42]

Thus, the manifestation of the absolute value as 'One Eternally Blissful Principle' represents the expression of the idea of God in everything as the expression of the impersonal principle of Unity in Diversities, "Unity in variety is the plan of the Universe. We are all men, and yet we are all distinct from one another."[43] The realisation of this unity in differences gradually expresses the supreme or universal existence of Unity as God: "That Universal existence is God, the Ultimate Unity in the Universe. In Him We are all one."[44] The development of this ultimate oneness establishes the final Unity in God, Man and Nature: "Infinity can only be one, undivided. Thus, the conclusion will be reached that the infinite is one and not many, and that one Infinite soul is reflecting itself through thousands and thousands of mirrors, appearing as so many different souls. It is the same Infinite Soul, which is the background of the universe, that we call God. The same Infinite soul also is the background of the human mind, which we call the human soul."[45]

Through this realisation of infiniteness, the individual man becomes free when immortal man comes out of his mortal and finite existence, what is the Universal Existence of man at the highest state of human freedom: "Freedom is inseparably connected with immortality. To be free one must be above the laws of nature. Law exists so long as we are ignorant. When knowledge comes, then we find that law is nothing but freedom in ourselves. The will can never be free, because it is the slave of cause and effect. But the "I" behind the will is free: and this is Self. "I am free" that is the basis on which to build and live. And freedom means immortality."[46]

This highest state of freedom as explained by Vivekananda, represents Tagore's idea of *'at-homeness' (Sarvanubhuti)* as the feeling of intimacy with everything. This transcendental experience has been analysed by Sri Aurobindo as "To become complete in being, in consciousness of being, in force of being, in delight of being and to live in this integrated completeness is the divine living."[47] Indeed there is a continues development of this advanced transcendent experience from Vivekananda to Tagore and from both to Sri Aurobindo.

The philosophy of man, as developed by these contemporary Indian thinkers, is a creative synthesis of materiality or finiteness and infiniteness in the finite existence of man in this world, developing a prospective programme for human freedom in unity as the spiritual expression of humanity as godness in different creative states of existence in different degrees. In the context of this humanistic outlook, Vivekananda's idea of man is evaluated by E.P. Chelishev thus: "In the sphere of this spirituality the thinker accentuated above all the position about the unity of immanent and transcendental spiritual source which served as the philosophical basis of its own kind of the category of greedlessness."[48] This type of the spiritual progress of man is to cultivate the spirit of detachment or "'greedlessness' through social process of love for developing the absolute spiritual value of goodness as pure Bliss or Unity among different contradictions due to egoistic and individualistic process of life. In the observation of Mr Chelishev, this process of developing human' unity "...as believed by Vivekananda, is achieved, in the process of realisation by man of his divine essence, the consciousness of the position that all people in their true essence are one. Here man's consciousness itself' of his divine essence already conditions, from Swamiji's point of view, the potential possibility of eradication of egoism."[49] So 'Eradication of egoism' according to Vivekananda, means to be free from all contradictions due to poor self or ego as individualism and on the other had it is to manifest the real Man as Infinite or the Spiritual Man in finite existence.

So this process of developing the spirituality in man is "... man's abstract realisation of his identity with Brahman."[50] It lies in the idea of abstract unity of the divinity and humanity as spiritual identity of man and God with the expression of the idea of concrete unity as humanistic value of goodness as godness in human existence. Mr Chelishev explains this spiritual process of developing man as 'Vital activity', which, in his observation, may be stated thus: "...a man, according to Vivekananda's notion, is impelled towards that stage of perfection which consists in the merging of the individual and the universal spiritual source."[51]

Notes and References

1. R.M. Maciver and Charles H. Page, *Society,* 1962, p. 172.
2. *Ibid,* p. 174.
3. Swami Ranganathananda, *Science and Religion,* 1982, p. 2.
4. Religion and Science, *Complete Works* of *Swami Vivekananda,* Birth Cent, Edn, 1963, Vol. VI, pp. 81-82.
5. *Ibid.,* p. 81
6. *Ibid.,* p. 82
7. S. Radhakrishnan, *Religion and Culture,* 1968, p. 2.
8. John Caird, *Introduction to the Philosophy* of *Religion,* 1956, p. 96.
9. *Ibid,* pp. 100-101.
10. Eddington, *Science and the Unseen World,* 1929, p. 54.
11. Teilhard de Chardin, *The Phenomenon* of *Man,* 1959, pp. 35-36.
12. Vivekananda, Religion is Realisation, *Complete Works* Swami of *Vivekananda,* Birth Centi Edn, 1963, Vol. VI, p. 82.
13. Vivekananda, What is Religion? *Ibid. Vol I,* p. 335
14. *Ibid,* p. 335.
15. Lincoln Barnett, *The Universe and* Dr. *Einstein,* 1950. p. 103.
16. *Complete Works* of *Swami Vivekananda,* Birth Cent. Edition, 1963, Vol. I, p. 336.
17. Rabindranath Tagore, Man's Universe, *The Religion* of *Man,* 1970 p. 9.
18. *Complete Works* of *Swami Vivekananda,* Birth Cent Edn, 1963 Vol II, pp. 64-65.
19. *Ibid.,* p. 57.
20. *Ibid.,* p. 59.
21. *Ibid.,* p. 63.
22. *Ibid.,* p. 75.
23. *Ibid.,* p.75.
24. *Ibid,* p. 75.
25. *Ibid,* p. 79.

26. Vivekananda, The Real Nature of Man, *Complete Works of Swami Vivekananda,* Birth Cent Edn, 1963, Vol. II, p. 80.
27. The Divinity of Man, *Complete Works of Swami Vivekananda,* Birth Cent Edn, 1963, Vol. III. p. 498.
28. *Ibid,* pp. 499-500.
29. Immortality, *Complete Works of Swami Vivekananda,* Birth Cent Edn, 1963, Vol. II, p. 236.
30. Realisation, *Ibid,* pp. 173-174.
31. *Ibid.,* p. 174.
32. *Ibid.,* p. 167.
33. Maya and lllusion, *Ibid,* p. 97.
34. Unity in Diversity, *Ibid,* p. 181.
35. The Absolute and Manifestation, *Ibid,* p. 130.
36. Discourses on Jnana-yoga, *Ibid,* Vol. VIll. pp. 3-4.
37. Tagore, *Dharma,* 1355 B.S.
38. *Complete Works of Swami Vivekananda,* Almora, 1951, Vol. VII. p. 72.
39. V.S. Kostyuchenko, *Philosophical Teaching of Swami Vivekananda,* Swami Vivekananda Studies in Soviet Union, 1987, p. 242.
40. *Ibid.,* p. 244.
41. *Ibid.,* Vol. II, p. 55.
42. The Freedom of the Soul, *Complete Works .of Swami Vivekananda,* Birth Cent Edn, Cal, 1763. Vol. II. p. 191.
43. *Ibid.,* p. 381.
44. *Ibid.,* p. 381.
45. Soul, Nature and God, *Ibid,* p. 431.
46. Freedom of the Self, *Ibid,* Vol. VI, p. 84.
47. Sri Aurobindo, *The Future Evolution of Man,* 1974, p. 131.
48. E.P. Chelishev, *Neo-Vedantist Ethics of Swami Vivekananda,* Swami Vivekananda Studies in Soviet Union, 1987, pp. 34-35.
49. *Ibid.,* p. 36.
50. *Ibid.,* p. 38.
51. *Ibid.,* pp. 38-39.

Part - II

Freedom through Unity in Tradition with Prospect

Philosophy of Man, The Spiritual, in the observation of Swami Vivekananda, is to develop the 'stage of perfection' as human freedom which may be evaluated as "...the merging of the individual and the universal spiritual source." This idea of merging of the individuality and universality is the unfoldment of the creative unity in different states of individual and collective existence of men in this world. Fundamental object of this process is to make man free from his outer and inner limits that finally leads to the development of unity in his collective state of existence as social freedom, in the background of "the universal spiritual source," as manifesting transcendental value of absolute unity. In the observation of V. S. Kostyuchenko, it may be explained thus: "the concept of *moksha* also undergoes a characteristic change; Vivekananda treats it not as an individual but as a collective 'liberation' attained at a definite stage of evolution of society. This enabled Vivekananda to raise the question of the need not only of 'inner' but also 'outer', not only individual but also social premises for achieving the ideal set by him. These included also the creation of minimum of material conditions making it possible for the masses to avoid hunger, poverty and disease and thereby assist the awakening spiritual interests in them."[1]

Thus, considering Vivekananda's idea of human freedom as unity it is found that it is to be developed in the collective or social life of man in this world in different stages, that leads to the social freedom of man in and through social unity and equality. These are understood from a transcendental perspective as developed by Vivekananda. Man, in social unity through love and service for mankind-as from the above transcendental background by Vivekananda from the Upanishads to the *Vedantic* ideas, developed to his time-gradually realises his pure Being as Man which is the realisation of the universality in the finite existence of the individual. In this process, man gradually tries to realise his highest state of life that leads to the *Spiritual Freedom* in unity in man, God and World.

It may be said in this connection that man, both in his mental and social life, can not fully realise the total nature of human freedom because the infinite value of life as unity cannot be fully exhausted in any finite stage of life and world. This superb experience in this context is evidently transcendental in character as already indicated and for this, Vivekananda brings in the idea of *Videha Mukti,* that is final liberation when the human soul becomes united with infinite, eternal and transcendental Absolute.

But, truth in man, according to Swamiji, is his struggle for acquiring freedom in this life. So how he tries to acquire freedom and how much it can be acquired and established in this life and society become true to man. This idea urges Swamiji to introduce the idea of *Jivan Mukti* that is the establishment of internal experience in this life and world.

For the development of this idea of enjoyment of activity with a continuous sense of freedom - and unrestrictedness - Swamiji has used the term *Yoga* that is the union of the human life with the infinite presence in him which is the inauguration of an integral experience, in and through his finite existence in this material world. Again in another sense *Yoga* prescribes some methods or ways that include both the process and the realisation of an integral experiential process in human existence through the expression of human freedom in unity. These methods of *Yoga* may be explained in different ways and *yoga* of different forms are concrete and practical exercises for acquiring powers in progress, which may be explained by Mr Kostyuchenko, "Vivekananda constantly stresses that the main "yogic ways" correspond to the peculiarities of the main psychological types of people, characterised by the possession of knowledge, emotions or willful impulses in the over-all dynamics of their psychological life."[2] Thus, in the background of different psychological peculiarities of individuals, different methods or "yogic ways" as related to those attitudes and temperaments, are prescribed for determining the right direction in achieving freedom in unity. In the observation of pravrajika Atmaprana, it may be stated thus, "To meet the needs of men of different temperaments the different paths of spiritual disciplines have been laid down. "Yoga means 'yoke', to join, that is to join the soul of man with the Supreme Soul or God." Thus, the worker or the *Karmayogin* realises his own divinity through work performed unselfishly; the emotional man or *bhakta* realises it through devotion and love for a personal God; the mystic or the *rajayogin* realises it through control of the mind, and the philosopher, *jnanayogin,* through knowledge.

"Besides temperament, the three instruments of knowledge, instinct, reason and inspiration help to determine the right path for the aspirant."[3]

(a) Jnana

This process stands on the development of knowledge or consciousness as the expression of the particular aspect of nature or the religion of man; "Religion is learning to play consciously."[4] This acquisition of conscious process of religion through yoga, explains the manifestations of the nature of knowledge in different stages of life towards the development of the highest state of Being. Vivekananda points out, "Knowledge is the parent of intuition, which like instinct, is also unerring; but on a higher plan. There are three grades of manifestation in living beings: (1) subconscious-mechanical, unerring; (2) Conscious-knowing, erring; (3) Super-conscious-intuitional, unerring; and these are illustrated in an animal, man and God. For the man who has become perfect, nothing remains but to apply his understanding. He lives only to help the world, desiring nothing for himself. What distinguishes is negative - the positive is ever wider and wider. What we have in common is the widest of all, and that is "Being".[5]

The knowledge of this pure Being is the realisation of the true nature of man, which is called self-realisation and this can only be possible through the discriminative knowledge which is "a form of spiritual discipline based mainly on philosophical discrimination between the real and the unreal, and the renunciation of the unreal."[6]

So Jnana-Yoga is the meditation or the realisation of the true nature of human existence through the process of discrimination. It is a separation from unreality or material 'ego' and a renunciation of limitations or contradictions caused by 'ego'. The freedom from one's egoistic consciousness leads one to establish the total experience of finite with the Infinite. Swamiji explains, "The Jnani's meditation is of two sorts: (1) to deny and think away everything we are not; (2) to insist upon what we really are- the Atman, the one Self-Existence, Knowledge, and Bliss. The true rationalist must go on and fearlessly follow his reason to its farthest limits. It will not answer to stop anywhere on the road. When we begin to deny, all must go, until we reach what cannot be thrown away or denied, which is the real "I". That "I" is the witness of the universe, it is unchangeable, eternal, infinite."[7] It is nothing but adopting Husserl's methods of eliminating the confronted till the transcendent subject is directly experienced. Husserl was a post-Hegelian phenomenologist, refuting Hegel's Abstract egoistic Idealism.

The realisation of this infinite 'I' is the realisation of the highest state of life that leads to salvation in two forms. Man as a discriminator- may discriminate his pure being from a transcendent perspective and eliminating the confronted experience- from life, mind, body and other unreal states or bondages of the world and thus may acquire freedom in the embodied state of life and finally the self, in the disembodied state that becomes ultimately free from wordly existence. The later process is purely transcendental, indescribable through any intellectual ways.

So, *Jnana-Yoga* stands on the method of discrimination, distinguishing the real from the unreal and eliminating the unreal through the development of pure knowledge of Reality or Self. This process is evaluated by Pravrajika Atmaprana thus, "Jnana-Yoga is for the reflective nature. By the process of discrimination, the *Jnani* leaves out of count one thing after another of the Universe, until he discovers the Essential Unity. When this point is reached he sees that there is but One Self in the Universe, of which the lower selves are but manifestations. This is Advaita realisation."[8] Modern thinkers, do not accept the importance of mere *Jnana-Yoga* as it is the partial realisation of the total nature of man that is the one-sided development of reason as the method of analysis. Sri Aurobindo introduces *integral-yoga* for a total and synthetic development of the human personality by a continuous yogic process, which is a transformation of one's basic personality beyond one's mentality to a supramental order. Thus, it is found that *Jnana-Yoga* may prepare the individual self for its freedom, through the process of discrimination of real from unreal and through the renunciation of unreality, still it is unable to develop the total or the integrated personality of man.

(b) Karma

It is a moral discipline-cultivation of a spirit of detachment, in a social environment, in which one may be placed or born with. A *karma-yogin* may live in a social milieu, but his art of living would consist in developing the humanitarian outlook, abandoning selfishness: "Selflessness alone will solve the problem. Religion comes with intense self-sacrifice. Desire nothing for yourself. Do all for others. This is to live and move and have your being in god."[9]

The growth of man to a higher being is possible through an act of selflessness. This is cultivating urge to be free from one's interested work for worldly happiness or *Ptavtitti,* and preparing him for others in renunciation or *Nivritti.* Vivekananda points out with a command as below: "...hold your life a sacrifice for the welfare of others; and if you choose the life of renunciation, do not even look at beauty and money and power."[10] This ideal of *karma-yoga,* developed by Vivekananda as a proper ideal of renunciation. It is explained by Mr Chelishev thus, "His ideal was that of a karma-yogi, personifying greedlessness, bold, courageous and strong character, and called upon to solve problems mainly of day-to-day life. In the process of active practical work the Karma-yogi must subdue pravritti and cultivate greedlessness in self."[11] So the ideal of a *Karma-yogin* does not reject his worldly existence, but on the other hand; it teaches him to kill the spirit of selfishness, in one's activity-process, in a social milieu. Vivekananda points out, "Do not give up the world, live in the world, imbibe its influences as much as you can, but if it be for your own enjoyment's sake work not at all."[12] Thus, in all worldly activities, the fundamental end of a *Karma-Yogin* is to develop the spirit of unselfishness. This spirit of activity also inspires both atheists, and theists, to work for others. This wider attitude in man urges him to think about the whole universe, beyond his limited self-interest, and this can only be possible through the development of a selfless outlook in man. In the words of Vivekananda, it may be stated thus: "Stand in that reverent attitude to the whole universe, and then will come perfect non-attachment. This should be your duty. This is the proper attitude of work. This is the secret taught by Karma-Yoga."[13] The 'perfect non-attachment' develops in man a sense of an integral consciousness, through which he expresses the infiniteness in him. Vivekananda observes. "All that unites with the universal is virtue; all that separates is sin. You are a part of the Infinite. This is your nature. Hence you are your brother's keeper."[14] Thus, the inner essence of *Karma-yoga* cultivates the spirit of unity that inspires man to work for others in society, developing socio-political harmony. Mr Chelishev evaluates the significance of this process, "The basic principle of Karma Yoga-the principle of greedless action-had been the focus of Vivekananda's attention. In his ethical views this principle was basically not simply a call for religious activity for the purpose of attaining spiritual-moral level at which the confluence with *Atman* takes place, but as a call for activity which for him had a definite, socio-political slant. "Let us work like brothers" wrote Vivekananda, "...the future of India, depends on our common efforts."[15]

This type of selfless humanitarian outlook of Vivekananda's *Karma-yoga* has a similarity with the unconditional, unselfish attitude of the *Karma-yoga* of *Bhagvad Gita,* as both these views inspire man to kill his self-interest for the development of the highest state of human freedom. Vivekananda writes, "Those who work without any consciousness of their lower ego are not affected with evil, for they work for the good of the world. To work without motive, to work unattached, brings the highest bliss and freedom. This secret of Karma-yoga is taught by the Lord Shri Krishna in the Gita."[16]

So *Karma-yoga,* as prescribed by Vivekananda and *Bhagvad Gita,* is unconditional as it is really for the selfless service for mankind, developing the spirit of unity among men. For this Prabrajika Atmaprana rightly observes, "Karma-yoga is the science of right action. It teaches a man to be in the world, but not of it, like the lotus leaf, whose roots are in the mud but which remains always pure. No one can escape the wheel of *Karma.* Every one must work in the universe. 'Karma-yoga', said Swamiji, 'shows the process, the secret and the method of doing it to the best advantage ... instead of being knocked about in this universe, and after long delay and thrashing, getting to know things as they are, we learn from *Karma-yoga* the secret of work, the method of work, the organising power of work. A vast mass of energy may be spent in vain, if we do not know how to utilise it. Karma-yoga makes a science of work.' The practice of self-abnegation is the ideal method, and realising selflessness is the goal. Thus, the Karma-yogin without the help of doctrine or theory, through mere work, solves the very same problem to which the *Jnani* applies his reason and inspiration, and the Bhakta, his love."[17]

But regarding this particular method of *Karma-yoga,* it may be noted that though it leads to freedom, still without the knowledge or *Jnana* about the reality or the differences between good and evil, man cannot work rightly, and again also without the ideal of love, man also cannot develop his selfless attitude for the service of mankind. So, mere action or *karma* without love and knowledge cannot lead to perfect freedom. *Karma-yoga,* therefore, is always linked up in one aspect with *Jnana-yoga,* and in another aspect with *Bhakti-yoga.*

(c) Raja

It is a psycho-physical method for the realisation of truth as freedom. Vivekananda says, "the science of Raja-yoga proposes to put before humanity a practical and scientifically worked out-method of reaching this truth."[18]

Mr Kostyuchenko also explains this process of achieving truth thus, "Vivekananda seeks to present raja-yoga as a science of 'control over inner nature'...Here he takes notice of the possibility of consciously regulating with the help of yogic methods certain physiological and psychic processes which usually escape such control."[19] Patanjali introduced this method of Yoga or Union as the physical and mental discipline for the cessation of the modifications of mind Chitta-*Yogashchittavrittinirodah.* These modifications are (a) *Pramana,* (b) *Viparyaya,* (c) *Vikalpa,* (d) *Nidra,* and (e) *Smriti.*

Pure self or *Purusa,* as reflected in these modifications of *chitta* passes through the five kinds of sufferings or *Klesha* in this world, which are (a) avidya or ignorance, (b) *asmita* or egoism, (c) *raga* or attachment, (d) *dvesa* or aversion, (e) *abhinivesha* or desire for life and fear of death.

For the cessation of sufferings and modifications of minds, *Yoga* advocates the control over the mind, the senses and the body. So it does not ignore the bodily existence of man, or does not want to destroy the body, but on the other hand it wants to develop the mental process of man in togetherness towards the realisation of the potential perfection in him. Vivekananda rightly observes, "The end and aim of all sciences is to find the unity; the one out of which the manifold is being manufactured, that one existing as many. Raja-yoga proposes to start from the internal world, to study internal nature, and through that, control the whole - both internal and external."[20] So the process of *Raja-yoga* may be explained as the self controlling process which is evaluated by Atmaprana thus: "Raja-Yoga is the science of 'restraining the chitta (mind) from breaking into Vrittis (modifications).' It thus teaches' concentration of mind and purification of intention. These ultimately make man free from the limitations of the senses and makes him transcend reason and thus reveal the potential divinity within. The control of chitta or the meditation is necessary in all the yogas and hence Raja-yoga can be said to be the basis of all of them."[21]

For the realisation of this highest state of unity or freedom, *Raja-yoga* prescribes the Eightfold paths of Discipline viz. *Yama, Niyama, Asana, Pranayama, Pratvahara, Dharana, Dhyana, Samadhi.* (I) *Yama* deals with five principles of conduct., e.g. (a) *ahimsa* or non-injury, (b) *Satya* or truthfulness, (c) *asteya* or non-covetiousness, (d) *brahmacharya* or passionlessness, (e) *aparigraha* or abstention from avarice. It is the control of the bodily processes. (2) *Niyama* is the cultivation of good habits that includes (a) *sauca* or purification of body and mind, (b) *santosa* or contentment, (c) *tapas* or austerity, (d) *svadhyaya* or study, (e) *Isvarapranidhana* or devotion to God. It is a discipline of an individual in a social milieu, for self-purification also involves a recognition and admission of one's confirmation to approve social ways. (3) *Asana* means the steady and comfortable posture of the body for-bodily discipline that includes *Padmasana, Virasana,* etc. It is a ground for controlling one's different parts of the body with a process of lifting it up to higher orders of organismic control. (4) *Pranayama* is the control of breath for the improvement of the conditions of body like blood circulation, function of heart etc. Here the control of one's breath, is not merely for the testing of the health condition of the body but, it is a ground for the control of the mental processes. (5) *Pratyahara* is the withdrawing of the senses from the external objects - the aim being to lift the organism from the basic to mental order, wherefrom the higher form of mental control will be effectively possible.

These five paths of Discipline are called external aids to Yoga or *bahiranga sadhana* and the remaining three are internal aids or *antaranga sadhana.* In yoga, these two processes go together. Yoga is an integral process, connecting the bodily processes through the breathing processes to higher processes of mind to reach the supra-mental orders. (6) *Dharana* is the fixing of the mind on the object of meditation. (7) *Dhyana* is the meditation or the steadfast contemplation without any disturbance. (8) *Samadhi* is concentration through which mind becomes identified with the object and thus in the highest state, mental modifications are ceased. The triadic mental disciplines of *Dharana, Dhyana* and *Samadhi,* generate powers in togetherness-which is *samyama.*

Samadhi is of two kinds: conscious or *samprajnata* when the consciousness of the object of meditations persists or *Ekagara,* and the latter stage is supra-conscious or *Asamprajnata* when there is no more any idea to confront, but only a transcendent condition to realise or develop progressively. It is the condition of suspension *(Niruddha)* of mental processes and modifications. Sharma explains this procedure, "If fire is restricted to a particular fuel, it burns that fuel alone: but when that fuel has been completely burnt, the fire also dies down. Similarly in conscious concentration, the mind is fixed on the object of meditation alone and modification arises only in respect of this object of meditation: but in supra-conscious concentration, even this modification ceases. It is the highest form of *Yoga* which is divine madness, perfect mystic ecstasy-difficult to describe and more difficult to attain. Even those who attain it can not retain it longer. Immediately or after very short time, the body breaks and they obtain complete liberation."[23] This deliberation of Sharma is one-sided. The real merge into *Asamprajnata* condition, is an absence of a restricted consciousness, but a confluence of Infinity of consciousness - it is a landing into an ocean of consciousness - or the sphere of unlimited *power-Kaivalya* condition of *yoga.*

Regarding this way of *Raja-Yoga* a deep rooted difficulty in it may be referred to. That is through the paths of this *Yoga,* a man may acquire a supernormal power that may develop the *Ego* in man through which he is tempted to exploit the common sentiment of people and thus finally he is deprived from acquiring the highest state of freedom in unity. But this aspect of yoga is the result of *Samprajnata yoga,* and not of the later stage of *Asamprajnata yoga.* Again according to some, it is an incomplete method or process, because without the knowledge or *Jnana* of Reality or self, as the object to be meditated, there can not be the meditation or *Yoga.* It is also an uncommon and extra-ordinary process that cannot be generally applied in human life. Still the highest value, deduced by this method through the knowledge of reality and renunciation of unreality, lies in the supreme Union or *Yoga* of finite with the Infinite in the State of freedom through a process of synthesis in knowledge and love. All these deliberations on *Yoga* have to be cultivated by a clear distinction between two types of *Yoga-Samprajnata* and *Asamprajnata.* No problem will arise when one rises to *Asamprajnata Yoga.* After the practice of the first three *yogas-jnana, karma,* and *raja-yoga,* one has to consider the *Bhakti-yoga.*

(d) Bhakti

It is a very common and natural process of life which is explained by Vivekananda as "the most natural way to reach the great divine and in view,"[23] through which man can develop his potential nature as love and thus expresses a deep devotion to God for the complete union in love, which is the highest state of freedom. Swamiji observes, "Bhakti-yoga is a real, genuine search after the Lord, a search beginning, continuing, ending in love. One single moment of the madness of extreme love to God brings us eternal freedom."[24]

Bhakti-Yoga is an easy method that can be exercised in and through activities and relations of men in their daily life. The feeling for others, potent in man as love, is gradually expressed in his service for others and thus develops in him a selfless attitude. This selfless expression is the expression of divinity in man when man takes everything as the expression of divinity that leads him to realize love as pure and unconditional and thus finally he realizes a complete unity as divinity. Vivekananda explains this evolutionary progress of love in man in different stages. He writes, "There are five stages of love. First, man wants help and has a little fear. Second, when God is seen as father. Third, when god is seen as mother. Then all men are looked upon as reflections of the Mother God. With the idea of Mother-God real love begins. Fourth, Love for Love's sake. Love for love's sake transcends all qualities. Fifth, Love in Divine Union. It leads to oneness or super consciousness."[25]

For the preparation of individual's life for the realisation of the highest state of love as an integral consciousness, unity, *Bhakti-yoga* prescribes some principles which are to be adopted in life and so are to be known as Preparatory Devotion or *Bhakti.* These are (a) *Viveka* or Purity in food (b) *Vimoha* or Freedom from desires, (c) *Abhyasa* or performance of religious practices, (d) *Kriya* or works for others, (e) *Anavasada* or cheerfulness. But all these realisations presuppose man's activity within a social milieu.

Through this preparatory process of *Bhakti* the supreme devotion of love or *Para-Bhakti* is developed that includes the disciplines of Renunciation of everything for love. Vivekananda points out, "Love itself is the eternal, endless sacrifice. You will have to give up everything. You cannot take possession of anything. Finding love, you will never want anything (else)...only be Thou my love for ever!"[26]

The realisation of this divine nature of love inspires man to see its universal existence in everything that is his realisation of God as the manifestation of love in everything: "...the Lord, is in every being, the wise have thus to manifest unswerving love towards all beings..."[27]

This Universal outlook leads to the self-surrender in man which is the suppression of the poor ego or limitations of life for the inauguration of the divinity in man through the manifestation of Infinite or Universal Love in him.

The lift to the Divinity in Man through the development of an integral experience in man makes him Divine and on the other hand, God as love and Bliss also becomes human as His divine existence is manifested in human life through the manifestation of the eternal or divine love in different stages, that can be recognised as the 'Human representations of the divine ideal of love.' The early stage of love is calm and peaceful which is called *Santa-Bhakti.* In the second stage God is loved as Master and devotee takes himself to be the servant of God, which is called *Dasya.* In the third stage of love God appears as friend, when He is taken as equal in position with man. This is called *Sakhya.* In the fourth stage of *Vatsalya* love, God is loved with full affection by man as his own child. Thus, through the manifestations of divine, love in different stages in different human forms in different degress, there will be the highest manifestation of love as sweet or *Madhura,* that establishes a sweet relationship between God and Man. This relation finally develops the perfect nature of Divinity when all the differences are to be fused into one. All these deliberations on Bhakti-yoga is elaborated in Indian thought from the stage of *Bhagvad Gita to Bhagavatas,* where the role of Sri Chaitanya of the sixteenth century is predominant.

In the analysis of different stages of love, in the final stage of developing divine oneness there will be the establishment of final freedom in Unity: "At last, love, lover and beloved become one. That is the Goal...Why is there any separation between soul and man, between soul and God?...Just to have this enjoyment of love. He wanted to love Himself, so He split Himself into many...This is the whole reason (or creation, says the lover, "We are all one. I and my father are one."[28]

This development of oneness or Unity as the Divine Union with Absolute in Love, in and through the differences, is consistently explained by Vivekananda that has a justification in its application on human life. Swamiji evaluates this process in the following manner: "We all have to begin as dualists in the religion of love. God is to us a separate Being, and we feel ourselves to be separate beings also. Love then comes in the middle, and man begins to approach God, and God also comes nearer and nearer to man. Man takes up all the various relationships of life, as father, as mother, as son, as friend, as master, as lover, and projects them on his ideal of love, on his God. To him exists as all these, and the last point of his progress is reached when he feels that he has become absolutely merged in the object of his worship. We all begin with love for ourselves, and the unfair claim of the little self make even love selfish. At last, however, comes the full blaze of light, in which this little self is seen to have become one with the Infinite. Man himself is transfigured in the presence of this Light of Love, and he realises at last the beautiful and inspiring truth that Love, the Lover, and the Beloved are one."[29]

In the process of developing oneness, Vivekananda's expiation and careful examination of the four ways of the realisation of Truth by *Jna-Yoga, Karma-Yoga, Raja-Yoga and Bhakti-Yoga,* prove that all these disciplined ways are to be exercised on the human life for the development of the diverse elements in men e.g. *Jnana, Karma, Bhakti* etc. from the diverse points of view.

Through these disciplines man gradually understands the integral relations among these diverse disciplined ways that transform one to a comprehensive outlook in life in confronting the apparent differences.

In the background of this ultimate ideal, we also find an integral development of man towards the highest transformed state. Thus, it may be said that though all these disciplined ways, if not developed in togetherness, may appear to be partial and incomplete, still this partiality or incompleteness can be removed through the establishment of the inter-relation among them from a comprehensive outlook. Vivekananda writes, "There is not really so much different between knowledge (*Jnana*) and love (*Bhakti*) as people sometimes imagine. We shall see, as we go on, that in the end they converge and meet at the same point. So also is it with *Raja-Yoga,* which when pursued as a means to attain liberation,...leads us also to the same goal."[30] All these unifying ways of the different forms of yogic disciplines have been indicated above.

The significance of this synthesis lies in the consistent application in human life through the introduction of love as developed through the pursuit of *Bhakti-Yoga* or *Yoga* of love. Regarding the nature of this ideal of love, Swamiji refers to, "This love can not be reduced to any earthly benefit", because so long as worldly desires last, that kind of love does not come; "*Bhakti* is greater than *Karma,* greater than *Yoga,* because these are intended for an object in view, while *Bhakti* is its own fruition, its own means and its own end."[31]

Thus, the realisation of this highest ideal of love in man is to realise the expression of his real nature as the manifestation of the pure being through the harmonious development of man's character in a systematic manner. Swamiji points out, "...We know that character is of the noblest type in which all these three knowledge and love and *Yoga* are harmoniously fused."[32] So the formation of man's character through the harmonious and systematic development of love finally paves the path for the social and integrated personality of man that urges him to realise the Reality, as an operative process of an integral self in him, through the renunciation of the restricted material ego, the construct of attachment, desires, limitations and contradictions of material world. So in developing integrated personality through *yoga* as synthetic process. Mr V. S. Kostyuchanko points out, "...this means that the system of influences on willful, emotional, and cognitive aspects of personality structures exhausts the possible means or re-orientation of individuals; but the essence of such re-orientation, from Vivekananda's point of view, must consist in reaching a 'spiritual balance' (*Samata*) and 'indifference to passions' (*vairagya*). Each of the Yogas attains this re-orientation in its own way, sometimes by inciting the will to denounce ego-centric urges (*karma-yoga*), sometimes by directing all emotions to one higher object (*bhakti-yoga*), sometimes showing the insignificance of the transient compared with the eternal (*jnana-yoga*).... But the Unity of the main yogas, according to Vivekananda, consists not only in the ultimate and (attainment of freedom) but also in the similarity of spiritual re-orientation made by them. These intertwine with each other, help each other; the combined operation of the three main forms of yoga is compared by Vivekananda with the co-ordination in the movement of two wings and tails in the flight of a bird....Here is hinted the idea of a single and "complete" yoga-purna-yoga, which was later developed in the works of Aurobindo Ghosh."[33]

Thus, in the socio-spiritual development of the idea and method of completeness, renunciation is the self-abnegation or the self-denial that is the sacrifice of the poor ego or selfishness for the welfare of the whole world. Service is the medium through which the ideal of renunciation becomes manifest, because this ideal can be realised through the selfless service for others. Again service without renunciation cannot be service for people in general, only the service with renunciation in various aspects and orders of social milieu can develop the personality of man in a harmonious manner that is the manifestation of the divine or selfless love in man through the disinterested service for others. Vivekananda explains the implications of the higher life through the renunciation and service in love in and through the practical procedure of man: "In practical daily life hurt by small things; we are enslaved by little beings. Misery comes because we think we are finite - we are little beings. And yet, how difficult it is to believe that we are infinite beings! In the midst of all this misery and trouble, when a little thing may throw me off my balance, it must be my care to believe that I am infinite. And the fact is that we are and that consciously or unconsciously all searching after that something which is infinite; we are always seeking for something that is free."[34] This pursuit of man in and through the contradictions of the material world, gradually transforms man to a free and universal outlook in him: "And in the midst of the depths of misery and degradation, the soul sends a ray of light, and man wakes up and finds that what is really his, he can never lose."[35] Thus, he realises the existence of the universal and Absolute value within him and also becomes universal and infinite: "Anger and lust and jealousy, evil thoughts and all these things, never come to me; for I am the Existence, the knowledge, the Bliss Absolute. I am it. I am it."[36] This vision of an integral consciousness in the existence of man through the harmonious development of his life in love, is also brought out by Rabindranath, when he observes, "It is not the magnitude of extension but an intense quality of harmony which evokes in us the positive sense of the infinite in our joy, in our love. For advaitam is anandam; the infinite One is Infinite Love."[37]

So, this philosophy of human life on the basis of the Ethics of Renunciation and Service in Love finally, expresses the eternal *divinity* in man as Man, The Spiritual when he realises,

"From highest Brahman to the yonder worm
And to the very minutest Atom,
Everywhere is the same God,
the All-Love;"[38]

In the context of this divine and spiritual outlook in its highest manifestation in cosmic and social process and pursuit towards the highest form of perfection or freedom, Man becomes Divine or Spiritual and God also becomes human. On account of this realisation Swamiji appeals,

"Friend! offer mind, soul, body, at their feet.
These are His manifold forms before the,
Rejecting them, where seekest thou for God?
Who loves all beings; without distinction,
He indeed is worshipping best his God."[39]

The inauguration of this idea of oneness or unity in diversities develops the philosophy of humanity which introduces the harmony among different states of individual and social existence with the introduction of value of oneness of divinity and humanity as unity of man, god and world.

Spiritual Development of the Religion of Humanity

The development of unity, in the observation of Vivekananda, is the expression of divinity or the inauguration of God in man which is the advancement of human life towards a spiritual process, beyond all limitations and contradictions. This superb experience is explained by Vivekananda, as below: "Man has wanted to look beyond, wanted to expand himself; and all that we call progress, evolution, has been always measured by that one search, the search for human destiny, the search for God."[40]

"The search for God", according to Vivekananda, is an essential part of the advancement of human adventure which is the proper goal of the religion of man as it accepts man as potentially divine and is manifest in an through this material world–process with all its restricted modes, which one has to transcend by continuous disciplines as suggested for the manifestation of goodness in man as the expression of human or social value of unity. In this process, Vivekananda evaluates the inner essence of religion on 'The Religion' or Oneness as Unity, signifying many religious sects with various restricted modes of life, expressing variety and plurality. But the real significance of religion as the religion of man, unfolding the potential human nature, lies in expanding unity is plural states of human existence.

Philosophically it may be observed that the manifestation of this Unity in the life of individual is the realisation of his Self as Oneness, when he realises his freedom in Unity as transformed integral consciousness through service to mankind, which has been well brought out by Swami Vivekananda and his glowing words are as below: "Man's free agency is established in the soul, and the soul, realising itself to be free, is always asserting the fact inspite of the mind's bondage: 'I am free! I am what I am! I am what I am! This is our freedom.'"[41]

The realisation of these consciousness of freedom in individual's social life becomes perfect and complete through his selfless service to mankind. In Swamiji's words, "The ultimate goal of all mankind, the aim and end of all religions, is but one–re-union with God, or what amounts the same, with the divinity which is every man's true nature."[42] But this is realise, as mentioned earlier by a selfless service and love, when love is disciplined expression in the social life of man, beyond all limitations.

So the life of the individual is to be free from the limitations and bondages through the realisation of his divine nature in love that becomes perfect through its manifestation in his collective or social life. This can be recognised as the final and fundamental end of all social ideals, religions and spiritualism. If the nature and significance of this aim is perfectly evaluated, it is found that the spirit of this end is to establish the perfect value of unity, which finally is taken as the ultimate state of Oneness or Absolute. But the significance of these oneness lies in its existence in man, who can realise it through the selfless procedure of life in society, that leads to the establishment of social unity. Thus, through the manifestation of the highest ideal of unity in the life of the individual, a man realises the existence of universality in him, beyond all limitations and contradictions of life and thus he becomes Universal Man or Divine. Again, through the application of this synthetic and universal outlook through the life and activates of individual, there will be the expression of divinity in society in different degrees that leads to the development of spiritual freedom as the divine life on earth.

This, according to Vivekananda, is the eternal or universal procedure of human life that can be recognised as proper expression of that true nature or religion of man, where material contradictions of human life and society cannot be ignored or rejected but are to be harmonised or synthesised through the introduction of the universal idea of Unity. Vivekananda explains the implication of the existence of this universal truth in religion, -"Each religion, as it were takes up one part of the great universal truth, and spends its whole force in embodying and typifying that part of the great truth. It is, therefore, addition, not exclusion. This is the idea. Systems after system arises, each one embodying a great idea, an ideals must be added to ideals. And this is the march of humanity."[43] This adventure towards a comprehensive process represents the real significance of the religions of the world in general. It leads to the development of comprehensive experiential process of the Universal Religion which includes the progress of humanity towards unity in all disharmonies or disunities. Regarding the meaning and significance of the Universal Religion of Man, Vivekananda points out, -"Religion is realisation; nor talk, nor doctrine, nor theories, however beautiful they may be. It is being and becoming, nor hearing or acknowledging; it is the whole soul becoming changed into what it believes. That is religion."[44] Religion is a process of transformation of one's personality by disciplined ways.

Thus, accepting religion as the natural development of human life by a disciplined life within a society with a march to other social processes, Vivekananda emphasises the human outlook of religion which stands on the life of man. But the real significance of this religion lies in its development of the broad humanist international outlook towards the universal unity. The significance of the humanistic process of developing unity as 'Supreme Truth' in the philosophy of life and existence, as examined by V. S. Kostyuchenko, "True, there are divergences even in the philosophy of religions, but these, as Vivekananda assumes, can be reduced to some basic points and presented in the form of steps leading to the single Supreme Truth. Thus, the attitude of man to God is thought of first as something external (God is the 'Supreme' Being different from us, the ruler of the world–the typical idea of The Old Testament), then as internal. God is in the hearts of people–the idea of the New Testament) and lastly, there is reached (in Advaita Vedanta) and understanding of complete identity of essence of man and God.... All religions, because of the presence of this 'Supreme Truth', their 'central point', can be presented in the form of an endless number or radii of circle converging into one point...."[45]

For the application or the realisation of this humanistic idea in life, Vivekananda also accepts human procedure, which according to him, is *Yoga* or Union. In this connection Vivekananda recognises different ways or *Yogas* for the development of different human qualities in different individuals, but the significance of this development lies in unity. Vivekananda explains this synthetic idea of *Yoga* in the analysis of the symbolic meaning of the seal of Ramakrishna Mission: "The wavy waters in the picture are symbol of *Karma,* the lotus of *Bhakti,* and the rising-sun of *Jnana.* The encircling serpent is indicative of *Yoga* and the awakened *Kundalini Shakti,* while the swan in the picture stands for the *Paramatman* (Supreme self). Therefore, the idea of the picture is that by the union of *Karma, Jnana, Bhakti* and *Yoga* the Vision of the *Paramatman* is obtained."[46] This *Pararmatman* is the realisation of the Universal self in man as Unity. The importance of this process of developing unity is explained by V. S. Kostyuchenko thus, "The fact that Vivekananda gave such great importance to 'Yogic practices', is not all just accidental. If Vedanta, from his point of view, establishes the ideal of freedom, the said four yogas are the ways to it. The very choice of these ways is quite significant. The fact is that these do not at all exhaust the whole diversity of the types of 'Yogic practices', existing in India. Vivekananda sometimes even writes about the 'infinite' ways of Yoga..."[47] The realisation of infinite as an end through the infinite means of realisation as infinite ways of yoga, refers to the synthetic development of life and society which is evaluated by Pravrajika Atmaprana, "By abandoning the safe paths of accepted ideals. Swamiji thus tried to work out this great contribution to the thought and practice of religion. The two philosophical problems about the concept of the Ultimate and the right mode of approach to it are still responsible for the creation of innumerable religions and religious sects in the world. For, these two problems are universal and all other problems can be grouped within their range. Swamiji's efforts to resolve the conflict by an appeal to reason, broad-mindedness and toleration may help the world today to work out some new realisation."[48]

The significances of this 'new realisation' as a process of synthesis in the philosophy of Swami Vivekananda, explains the practical and social implication of yoga through the realisation of inter-relatedness in realisation in love; as Vivekananda observes, "Love itself is the eternal, endless sacrifice. You will have to give up everything. You cannot take possession of anything. Finding love, you will never (want) anything (else)..."only be Thou my love for ever."[49] Thus, the absolute value as unity in love, is expressed through the human life as the human value in love, that again is manifested in society through the selfless love and the unconditional service for others. This process, in the observation of Gobinda Chandra Dev, is the basis of Vivekananda's ethics which stands on the renunciation of poor self or narrow interest through the inauguration of Universal Self as Unity in selfless love and service. He points out, "This emphasis on the positive content of renunciation brings into bold relief the other aspect of Vivekananda's Ethics, by far the more important aspect of it, viz. the idea of love and service, more particularly the idea of human service in the broadest sense.... In this philosophy of unity which is as much a content of his realisation as of his rich, spiritual heritage, Vivekananda finds the rationale of his Ethics of universal love and service."[50]

This synthetic procedure of developing universality in 'universal love and service', expresses the social implication of the ideal of interrelatedness which is manifested through the social life in a harmonious manner. The establishment of synthesis or harmony is also the fundamental end of Vivekananda's Universal Religion that develops an intimate relation or intercommunication among all religions of the world. Swamiji explains, "We see various forms of religion in the world. It is a bewildering study, but it is not, as many of us think, a vain speculation. Amidst this chaos there is harmony, throughout these discordant sounds there is a note of concord, and he who is prepared to listen to it will catch the tone." In this process, the social progress towards harmony in and through differences among different religions of the world is discerned. Vivekananda thinks of a common perspective in the international plan of life in all religions of the world, where "...each nation has a mission of its own to perform in this harmony of races..."[51] This type of attitude and outlook, may be the guiding principle of developing world community in modern world. MacIver and Page, two noted sociologists, explain the possibility of expanding this idea through a social process, "As civilised beings, we need the smaller as well as the larger circles of community. The great community brings us opportunity, stability, economy, the constant stimulus of a richer, more varied culture. But living in the smaller community we find the nearer, more intimate satisfactions. The larger community provides peace and protection, patriotism and some time war, automobiles and the radio. The smaller provides friends and friendship, gossip and face-to-face rivalry, local pride and abode. Both are essential to the full life process."[52]

Regarding the social significance of this "full life process" as the expression of the universal ideal of unity or harmony, Vivekananda explains its implication in a spiritual manner, where unity as an absolute value or ideal is taken as the goal of life which is to be developed in human life and society in different degrees in and through differences and contradictions. Vivekananda explains, "Unity in variety is the plan of the universe. We are all men, and yet we are all distinct from one another. As a part of humanity I am one with you, and as Mr So-and-so I am different from you. As a man you are separate from the woman; as a human being you are one with the woman. As a man you are separate from the animal, but as living beings man, woman, animal, and plant are all one, and as existence, you are one with the whole universe. That universal existence is God, the ultimate unity in the universe. In him we are all one."[53]

So oneness or unity in the sense of a comprehensive or integral vision in human life, is not the universal outlook in the higher orders of experiential developments- where positive contributions of different elements in men, towards the development of interrelatedness, are accepted. This, according to Swamiji, is the perfect process of life on earth which is explained by him: "It is the only joyful state of existence. Life on the plane of the spirit is the only life, and let us all try to attain to this realisation."[54] It is an experience of co-presence of all orders of experience with a pursuit towards a beyond.

So, the realisation of the "joyful state of existence" is a prospect beyond all apparent differences of human life and society that manifests the proper spirit of Vivekananda's Universal Religion of Humanity. It is a process of expressing universality as possible unity in diversities which is evaluated by Swami Ranganathananda as "...revealing the infinite possibilities that lie hidden in every human being and that need to be unfolded and manifested in course of man's life and work."[55] This humanistic way establishes the humanistic process of developing human freedom consisting of unity which explains the significance of the philosophy of Man, the Spiritual as the comprehensive development of universality in life and existence.

In the observation of Professor Sarkar we may finally evaluate this process in the following way. This comprehensive programme of Vivekananda, Sarkar points out, is the development of 'Unitive Vision' which, he thinks, '...is an expression of a disciplined and detached mind' that in his opinion, '...is the attainment of true freedom'. He examines this idea thus: "It is the inspiring background for operation in the divine way to serve mankind with love and a genuine sense of non-difference. Hence through this Unitive

Consciousness, which is obviously supramental, if one is operative, one can prescribe a life in togetherness, with a full realisation of brotherhood of mankind, admitting the legitimate place of differences in manners, customs and religious ideas that one inherits by one's birth in a country. Man also differs in his racial background, in health, wealth, education and culture, dress, food habits, likes and dislikes. Those are basic urges, but a rise to religious consciousness by the four-fold disciplines, is a willing transformation for rising beyond one's indisciplined mind, attached to confronted orders of experience. It is a life within a new family, with a sense of discipline and restraint as described in the life of the householder, according to Hindu tradition. This project of Swami Vivekananda confirms farther. Vivekananda's admission of the confronted world as real, and not as a kind of secondary order of reality (*Maya*) as indicated by Sankara in the past, in his interpretation of *Vedanta*. Vivekananda modifies this process, philosophically and religiously, and hence the removal of miseries or sorrows from all points of views is a practical necessity to inaugurate a new and vital social process, in a supramental order. In such a lifting process of rising human nature to a divine order, which is a concrete service to mankind as a whole, lies the fundamentals of all religions. This is a pursuit which all religious persons can follow, from their different religious heritage. It is undoubtedly and objective to be recommended to all religions of the world. Indeed, Swami Vivekananda, by suggesting all these possibilities, could virtually claim for himself a title of one who brought in a novel international religion, eliminating from it the claims of any exclusive religion, except as a pathway for rising to a supramental religious consciousness."[56]

The significance of '.....pathway for rising to a supramental religious consciousness' as suggested by Sarkar, lies properly in developing the religion of humanity in a novel international religion which may be evaluated as a humanistic process of cultivating the transcendental value of Unity in '....a new and vital social process, in a supramental order' with the experiential processes or reconciling diversities in different states of freedom, developing inter-cultural relation in harmony.

Notes and References

1. V.S. Kostyuchenko, *Conception of Neo-Vendantism,* Swami Vivekananda Studies in Soviet Union, 1987, p. 200.
2. *Ibid.*, p. 253.
3. *Swami Vivekananda Centenary Memorial Volume,* 1963, p. 303.
4. Jnana Yoga, *Complete Works of Swami Vivekananda,* Birth Cent. Edn., 1963, p. 270.
5. *Complete works of Swami Vivekananda,* Birth Cent. Edn., 1963, Vol. VIII, pp. 17-18.
6. Swami Nikhilananda, *Vivekananda-A Biography,* 1953, p. 212.
7. *Complete works of Swami Vivekananda,* Birth Cent. Edn., 1963, Vol. VIII, p. 4.
8. *Swami Vivekananda Centenary Memorial Volume,* 1963, p. 304.
9. *Complete works of Swami Vivekananda,* Birth Cent. Edn., 1963, Vol. VI, p. 83.
10. *Complete works of Swami Vivekananda,* Sixth Edn., Almora, 1956, Vol-I, p. 49.
11. E.P. Chelishev, *Neo-Vedantist Ethics of Swami Vivekananda,* Swami Vivekananda studies in Soviet Union, 1987, p. 37.
12. *Complete Works of Swami Vivekananda,* Almora, 1965, Vol. I, p. 81.
13. *Complete Works of Swami Vivekananda,* Birth Cent. Edn, 1963, Vol. V, p. 246.
14. *Ibid*, Vol. VI, p. 83.
15. E.P. Chelishev, *Neo-Vedantist Ethics of Swami Vivekananda,* Swami Vivekananda Studies in Soviet Union; 1987, pp. 36-37.
16. *Complete Works of Swami Vivekananda,* Birth Cent. Edn, 1963, Vol. V, p. 249.
17. *Swami Vivekananda Centenary Memorial Volume,* 1963, pp. 303-304.
18. *Ibid*, Vol. I, p. 128.
19. *Swami Vivekananda Studies in Soviet Union,* 1987, p. 256.
20. *Complete Works of Swami Vivekananda,* Birth Centinary Edition, 1963, Vol. I, p.133.
21. *Vivekananda Centenary Memorial Volume,* 1963, p. 303.
22. Chandradhar Sharma, *A Critical Survey of Indian Philosophy,* 1964, p. 173.
23. Bhakti Yoga, *Complete Works of Swami Viveksnende,* Birth Cent. Edn., 1963, Vol. III, p. 32.
24. *Ibid*, p. 31.
25. *Ibid*, Vol. VI, p. 90.

26. *Ibid.*, Vol. VI, p. 76.
27. *Ibid.*,Vol. III, p. 82.
28. Divine Love, *Ibid,* Vol. VI, p. 77.
29. *Ibid*, Vol. III, p. 100
30. *Ibid*, Vol. III, p. 32.
31. *Ibid*, pp. 31-32.
32. *Ibid*, p. 33.
33. *Swami Vivekananda Studies in Soviet Union,* 1987, pp. 253-254.
34. *Ibid*, p. 399.
35. *Ibid*, p. 401.
36. *Ibid*, p. 402.
37. Tagore, *The Religion of Man,* 1970, pp. 40-41.
38. Vivekananda, To a friend, *Complete Works of Swami Vivekananda,* Birth Cent. Edn., 1963, Vol. IV, p. 496.
39. *Ibid*, Vol. II, p. 359.
40. *Ibid*, Vol. VI, p. 35.
41. *Complete Works of Swami Vivekananda,* Fourth Edition, Vol. V. p. 219.
42. *Complete Works of Swami Vivekananda,* Birth Cent. Edn, 1963, Vol. II, p. 365.
43. *Ibid.*, p. 396.
44. *Swami Vivekananda Studies in Soviet Union,* 1987, p. 229.
45. *Complete Works of Swami Vivekananda,* Birth Cent. Edn. 1963, Vol. VII, p. 204.
46. *Swami Vivekananda Studies in Soviet Union,* 1987, p. 252.
47. *Vivekananda Centenary Memorial Volume,* 1963, p. 305.
48. *Complete Works of Swami Vivekananda,* Birth Cent. Edn. 1963, Vol. VI, p. 76.
49. *Vivekananda Centenary Memorial Volume,* 1963, p. 333.
50. *Complete Works of Swami Vivekananda,* Birth Cent. Edn. 1963, Vol. II, p. 371.
51. R.M. MacIver and Charles H. Page, Society, 1962, p. 11.
52. *Complete Works of Swami Vivekananda,* Birth Cent Edn, Vol. II, 1963, pp. 381-82.
53. *Ibid*, pp. 381-82.
54. *Ibid*, p. 174.
55. Swami Ranganathananda, *Swami Vivekananda, His Humanism,* Moscow University Lecture, 1982, p. 8.
56. Anil K. Sarkar, *Swami Vivekananda's Philosophy of Religion-Its Intercultural prospects* (An observation on The Spiritual Man by S.N. Chattopadhyay), May 1, 1985, California, U.S.A.

Chapter – 3

Swami Vivekananda's Ideas and Ideals: A Critical and Comparative Evaluation

Part - I

An Examination of Swamiji's Philosophy of Man

Religion is the primary basis of the Indian way of life and thus becomes the guiding spirit of contemporary Indian philosophy and culture. Swami Vivekananda, a great contemporary Indian thinker and a reformer, tries to develop his reformative outlook through the establishment of a new progressive idea of religion as the expression of the essential and eternal spirit of divinity in man. Religion, in this sense, is taken by him, not as an imposition of idea, but as an essential part of human life which is nothing but the expression of human nature. For the introduction of the dynamic and synthetic human outlook, his religion may be called as the religion of man, which may be recognised as the expression of Man, The Spiritual.

But if this religious philosophy of Man, The Spiritual of Vivekananda is carefully examined, there may arise some misunderstandings about his interpretation of religion, which, it may be said, are also to be evaluated in the background of the wider view as suggested by him towards a harmonious development of human life.

It may be argued that though Vivekananda's idea of religion may be stated in leading to an international and intercultural prospect of Religion of Man, it stands on the synthetic development of the universal existence of man which tries to harmonise ideals of different religions and cultures of the world, yet his idea of religion is primarily based on *Hinduism*. It includes the spiritual outlook of *Vedas* and

Upanishads and also introduces the Hindu way of life in his religious system that stands on the traditional *Hinduism* or *Indian Spiritualism*. So in this context, it may be noted here that though Swamiji speaks of Universal Religion of Humanity, yet his religion is rooted in the Hindu religious traditions of India in a liberal sense and in development.

Now, if the significance of the term *Hinduism* as used by Vivekananda is explained, this misunderstanding regarding the nature of his religion as *Hinduism* does not arise. *Hinduism* is not taken by him as a code or any rigid regulation to be imposed upon man from without but it is the history of the progress of man that stands on the development of human life from within, which is the manifestation of the infiniteness in man towards a balanced development of all differences and contradictions in life and society in a progressive direction. Swamiji points out, "The Hindus found their creed upon the ancient Vedas, a word derived from Vid, 'to know'. These are a series of books which, to our minds, contain the essence of all religions; but we do not think they alone contain truths. They teach us the immortality of the soul. In every country and every human breast there is a natural desire to find a stable equilibrium, something that does not change."[1]

So Vivekananda puts an emphasis on the universal spirit of *Hinduism* that includes the integral consciousness which continuously leads one to advance in the direction of a broad social life with 'a stable equilibrium'. Thus, it may be said that *Hinduism* accepts different human values of different religions of the world as items for novel deliberations which refer to the infinite varieties of man's life. Swamiji observes, "...We not only tolerate, but we the Hindus accept every religion, praying in the mosque of the Mohammedans, worshipping before the fire of the Zoroastrians, and kneeling before the cross of the Christians, knowing that all religions, from the lowest fetishism to the highest absolutism, mean so many attempts of the human soul to grasp and realise the infinite, and each of them marking a stage of progress."[2]

This prospective and integral outlook of *Hinduism* makes it a comprehensive process, because from the lowest stage of idolatry with its mythologies to the development of the highest stage of absolute unity as introduced by *Advaita Vedanta*, it evaluates different ways of life and religion e.g. *theism, atheism*, etc. and thus broadens the eternal outlook of all religions towards the development of a universal consciousness, and importance of all religions. In this process of development, the image or idol worship of *Hinduism* is introduced in the first stage of the common life for the concentration of the mind on the idea of unity as God in man that finally leads him to realise his highest state of life when he realises his freedom in unity. In this Hindu way of religion, though a man may start from idol worship, still this way may lead to the development of the spirit of unity through the realisation of absolute value in and through different varieties of human life. Vivekananda writes, "The Hindus have discovered that the absolute can only be realised, or thought of, or stated through the relative; and the images, crosses, and crescents are simply so many symbols, so many pegs to hang the spiritual ideas on. It is not that this help is necessary for every one, but those that do not need it have no right to say that it is wrong. Nor is it compulsory in Hinduism."[3] Thus, this process, though is not necessary or compulsory, still it can help a man in realising unity in differences. This stage of realisation, according to different religious faiths, is the highest realisation of God as Unity. So the inclusion of this highest stage of realisation in *Hinduism* develops its universal philosophical outlook that introduces an integrated idea in different religious faiths of the world. After a careful examination of this universal spirit of *Hinduism*, Vivekananda explains the significance of the application of this wider outlook in religion and thus points out, "...if there is ever to be a universal religion, it must be one which have no locations in place or time, which will be infinite, like the God it will preach, and whose sun will shine upon the followers of Krishna and of Christ, on saints and sinners alike, which will not be Brahmanic or Buddhistic, Christian or Mohammedan, but the sum total of all these, and still have infinite space for development which in its catholicity will embrace in its infinite arms and find a place for every human being; from the lowest groveling savage not far removed from the, brute, to the highest man towering by the virtues of his head and heart almost above humanity...It will be a religion...which will recognise divinity in every man and woman, and whose whole scope, whose whole force will be centred in aiding humanity to realise its own true, divine nature."[4]

For the development of the consciousness of the divine nature of each man, Vivekananda accepts also the different disinterested ways for its realisation in life. For this, he interprets the Hindu view of *Yoga* as Union a disciplined way in several aspects as to discover the inner essence of Man's nature and his activity process. This is the expression of different elements of men through different ways or *Yogas* which are to be synthesised through disinterested service in selfless love of man for the development of universality or infiniteness in man, beyond the limitations of life. This process of unconditional love and selfless service, makes man to reveal his eternal oneness as universal unity with all that is free from any restriction of *Hinduism* or other limitations and divisions of life.

In this light of universality in man and religion, another misunderstanding about Vivekananda needs to be cleared. A charge against Vivekananda is that as he is a *Vaidantik Sannyasi,* he accepts the idea of *Advaita Vedanta* which observes that *Brahman* or Absolute is the only reality and this world is mere illusion. For this, Vivekananda, being a *Vedantist*, accepts that Absolute is the only reality and thus takes the way of life of a monk or *Sannyasi* for the renunciation of the material world which may be interpreted as unreal.

But the inner implication of Swamiji's interpretation of the idea of *Vedanta* and its practical application in the life of man in this material world prove the significance of the teaching of Vivekananda, that lies in the practical implication of *Vaidantic* ideal as non-duality or unity, which, through its application in human life, establishes Swamiji's neo-*Vedantic* outlook of the religion of man.

Now, it is to be noted in this connection, that Swamiji does not ignore the existence of man in this world, his denial is of the limitations or contradictions in man due to material ego or arrow self interest. These, in the observation of Vivekananda, are to be reconciled through the development of human life, which shows that the truth in man lies in the fighting against these evils or contradictions, and finally these are to be harmonised in and through the manifestation of infinite ideal of unity in man and in this world. This is the introduction of the neo-Vedantic outlook of Vivekananda, and so he observes, "The Vedanta preaches the ideal, and the ideal, as we know...There are two tendencies in human nature: one to harmonise the ideal with the life, and the other to elevate the life to the ideal."[5]

Thus, through the application of *Vedantic* disciplines through *yogic* practices, there is a harmonious development of man and society through which both the orders of Nature are raised to a prospective level where man's activity is a great need. This is the practical or moral approach of *Vedanta* that urges man to suppress his short-sighted egoistic cravings or attachments for them. They are just preliminary needs for sustenance of one's body or mind. But man has to develop himself towards a realisation of his divinity as the undeniable element in him for his further progress is the life of his self from the confronted situation of a material and a social universe. In this context, Vivekananda tries to justify the significance of the application of *Vedanta* in modern world and points out, "This practical side of Vedanta morality is necessary as much today as it ever was, more necessary, perhaps, than it ever was, for all this privilege–claiming as become tremendously intensified with the extension of knowledge... The difference between God and the devil is nothing except in unselfishness and selfishness. The devil knows as much as God, is as powerful as God; only he has known holiness that makes him a devil. Apply the same idea to the modern world; excess of knowledge and power, without holiness, makes human beings devils...That is why *Vedanta* wants to preach against it, to break down this tyrannising over of the souls of men."[6] Man's disciplines should be more than before for the confronted Universe with its science and technological facilities are more tempting than the assets of the past.

Thus, according to Swamiji, the holiness or unselfishness, in the heart of man, is God in man that signifies His continuous presence in society through the elimination of attachment for growing facilities and possessions provided by this industrial civilisation, and in this way man realises absolute value of non-duality as Knowledge, Bliss and Existence. Regarding this realisation Vivekananda observes,

"Man manifests knowledge, discovers it within himself, which is pre-existing through eternity. Everyone is the embodiment of knowledge, everyone is the embodiment of Eternal Bliss and Existence. The ethical effect is just the same, as we have seen elsewhere, with regards to equality."[7] Man's knowledge is no longer just individual's cognizance, it is a growing process of cognizance in different aspects and orders of the confronted universe.

Thus, "with regard to equality" or in relation to the introduction of unity in life and society, Swamiji finally accepts the *advaita* view of non-duality of God and Man, through which God as the height value of unity is manifested through the human life and society in this world. According to the dualistic sects of India, the individual souls remain as individuals throughout, and God creates the universe out of pre-existing material only as the efficient cause. According to the *Advaitists*, on the other hand God is both the material and the efficient cause of the universe. His not only the creator of the universe, but He creates it out of Himself. That is the Advaitist position.[8] So, this neo-vedantic outlook of Vivekananda does not reject this world as unreal because the Ultimate Reality or God is manifested through world as the materials and the efficient cause of the world. But on the other hand the apparent contradictions in the material world, are finally harmonised in the highest Reality as Unity. What is important is not merely his non-dualist ideas, nor even his acceptance of the confronted Universe and its importance as arena of man's activity, but the possibility of the expression of the universal religious consciousness which links up all aspects and orders of experience to a prospect along with man's discovery of divinity in himself. It is operative though this elevated process, where no longer there remains the religious differences, but they become just varied confrontations to be faced and directed towards a further prospect.

Swamiji points out that this universal spirit is present in all religions, that is to be developed towards a common goal. He writes, "The Bible, the Vedas, the Koran and all other sacred books are but so many pages and an infinite number of pages remain yet to be unfolded. I would have it open for all of them. We stand in the present but open ourselves to the infinite future. We take in all that has been in the past, enjoy the light of the present and open every window of the heart for all that will come in the future."[9] This means that through a continuous development of the views of different religions, the narrow outlook of religions will be changed and a new form of synthetic and universal religion will be evolved, which makes the proper use of religion with the growth of different sciences, extending the scope and spheres of knowledge. Swamiji explains, "Therefore, religions will have to broaden. Religious ideas will have to become universal, vast, and infinite, and then alone we shall have the fullest play of religion, for the power of religion has only just begun to manifest in the world...The power of religion, broadened and purified, is going to penetrate every part of human life. So long as religion was in the hands of a chosen few or of a body of priests, it was in temples, churches, books, dogmas, ceremonials, forms, and rituals. But when we come to the real, spiritual, universal concept, then, and then alone, religion will become real and living; it will come into our very nature, live in our every movement, penetrate every pore of our society, and be infinitely more a power for good than it has ever been before."[10] There is a need for knowledge not alone of past religious ideas, except its disciplines, but ways and means to let religion go side by side with the growing and multiplying sciences.

Thus, through the evolution of this proper idea of religion as not one of confining one to its abstract ideas, but as one of the experiential processes in development, Vivekananda discovers a new human outlook in *Hinduism* and *Advaita Vedanta*, that does not introduce any dogmatic code of life, but on the other hand it develops a new outlook of the universal applicability of religious experience in concrete human situation, its need is only on the side of a discipline. Regarding this new spirit of *Hinduism* and *neo-vedantic* religion as disciplined ways of life. Vivekananda observes, "With the Hindus you will find one national idea-spirituality....They tried to define the ideal of soul so that no earthly touch might mar it. The spirit must be divine;...The same idea of unity, of the realisation of God, the omnipresent, is preached throughout. They think it is all nonsense to say that He lives in heaven, and all that. It is mere human, anthropomorphic idea."[11] The religious ideas are for a personal discipline and not for dogmatising upon some abstract ideas pertaining to a specific religion.

This broad human outlook of religion is introduced by Vivekananda for the development of man's sphere of activity in mutuality, with an allowance of coexistence with same importance. Vivekananda finally expresses the infinity or divinity of Man that makes Him equally important as the cherished God-consciousness of the past. Now this consciousness is transferred to all to be enjoyed equally with freedom. In this development of the idea of the divinity in man. Swamiji firstly introduces the theistic outlook of personal God when man gradually realises the divinity in different degrees and God is also manifested in human life in different degrees and thus in this way the highest form of affinity is established in Man and God through the introduction of Swamiji's idea of *Absolutism* or *Advaita* idea of non-duality. So, in this extended explanation of the nature of man and God, Swamiji reconciles the ideas of *Theism* and *Absolutism*, and thus meets the charge against him: "...Vivekananda fails to reconcile theism with absolutism. The conception of God as personal and impersonal, determinate and indeterminate, creative and transcendental require adequate reconciliation. The theistic element is absent in Vivekananda's philosophy. In his thought, God as a supreme personal being has no reality. There is, therefore, no question of reconciliation between the Absolute and the unreal God. The metaphysician, therefore, escapes from solving the problem of reconciliation."[12] Vivekananda's discovery of God or divinity in man, is an incentive of love and service for man, religious experience is no more a matter for abstract discourse of the past.

Swamiji's explanation of the ideas of divinity is the idea of personal God, as manifested in human life in the forms of human values that leads to the realisation of the transcendental idea of the Absolute Unity. It may be pointed out that the total nature of God as Absolute Value of Unity is not fully manifested in any particular stage of human life and society. It is a process of manifesting the different aspects of Absolute Value in different stages of life towards the final realisation of the perfect state of Absolute Unity. For this, Vivekananda introduces the ideal of *Absolutism* that urges man to transcend his limitations for the development of his infinite potentiality towards the realisation of his perfect state of life as unity. Swamiji carefully explains the significance of this idea, "We believe in God, the father of the universe, infinite and omnipotent. But if our soul at last becomes perfect, it also must become infinite. But there is no room for two infinite unconditional beings, and hence we believe in personal God, and we ourselves are He. These are the three stages which every religion has taken. First, we see God in the far beyond, then we come nearer to Him and give Him omnipresence, so that we live in Him; and at last we recognise that we are He."

Now it is to be noted in this connection that a man through the realisation of his potential infiniteness, becomes divine which is explained by Vivekananda, as the presence of God in man. This type of the divinity of man as a disciplined experience operative through love and service of every distressed personality with a complete detached attitude, is present in different systems of philosophy. Particularly the contemporary Indian thinkers, like Sri Aurobindo and Rabindranath also accept the divinity in man. But according to Sri Aurobindo, man in this state of continuous development and transformation of ascent beyond mental orders, has the capacity to rise to the level of gnostic being which is a supramental function. Rabindranath observes the descent of universality in man through the evolution of divinity in man. Iqbal also accepts the change of prophet souls in the development of divinity in man. So, all these thinkers of the present century introduce a new outlook of religious consciousness and philosophy of man, quitting the past immobile idea of some kind of abstract idea of God.

In the context of evaluation of the philosophy of divinity as the perfect humanity, developed by Vivekananda with other contemporary Indian thinkers, we may also examine and can remove the charge against him that he may not be recognised as a progressive thinker or philosopher, for he has repeated and reestablished the traditional Indian view and *Advaita* idea in his thoughts and activities.

But a careful examination of Vivekananda, proves that his progressiveness lies in the analysis of his idea of religion of man, which, in his observation, is not the imposition of some traditional thoughts or ideals upon man, but it, on the other hand, is the natural expression of the divine nature of man as Man, The Spiritual. So in this way, he evaluates the divine nature of man, in a very natural form and thus shows that the essence of divinity lies in its significant expression in social life. This proves that a man, though exists individually his true individuality develops the spirit of interrelatedness with others that finally introduces the idea of unity with all. This is universal in nature and can also be developed in a universal process of love and service for mankind that makes a man free from limitations and contradictions in different degrees with the introduction of the state of perfection as the development of ideal of freedom in unity.

This humanistic and progressive development of the philosophy of Vivekananda, introduces the idea of unity in a perfect sense as it synthesises the ideals of humanity with divinity in a synthetic development of neutral, social and spiritual states of human freedom in unity which finally inaugurates the spirit of non-duality or oneness as *Advaita.* So this spiritual process of Vivekananda is a social and practical approach of *Advaita* outlook in traditional and universal or dynamic and synthetic form, which may thus be recognised as the *neo-vedantic* or practical *vedantic* and progressive philosophy of Vivekananda.

It may be observed further that this social, universal or progressive view of Vivekananda also denounces the individualistic attitude of particular religion and philosophy for attaining freedom for particular individual with individualistic process. But Vivekananda's philosophy of man, may be recognised as the religion of man as Man, The Spiritual which is a socio-spiritual outlook of developing universality in a socio-spiritual process of *yoga* as Union, developing social and universal idea of human freedom in unity.

The fundamental end of Vivekananda's religion of Man, The Spiritual, is the achievement of social freedom that can be made possible through the development of *Humanism* in religion, where freedom of individual man becomes complete through the freedom of men in society. In the observation of Vivekananda this process is spiritual in nature as there is the descent of God in man, and developing a new social service which is religiously oriented.

The gulf between God and man is resolved. Man's sphere of activity is essentially and also deeply human.

In this human process, Vivekananda's insistence on perfection of man through the disciplined ways of various *yogas* from *Jnana* to *Bhakti Yoga,* is a concrete step with an appreciation of an earned capacity in social situation. Here one can see the play of knowledge, activity, discipline - as love and service in full sway the whole sphere of being this - worldly and widely social and humanist.

The harmonious development of individualities or different elements in men through the inauguration of universality towards the establishment of social freedom in unity, is the fundamental end of Vivekananda's idea of *Humanism* in religion where he prescribes a social and synthetic method of selfless love and unconditional service for mankind, that, in one hand unites all methods of realisation of different elements which are to be synthesised in men and in the other hand, harmonises all these elements for the development of unity in life and society and thus finally; Swamiji observes a highest state of freedom in absolute non-duality is to be realised. This is the social outlook of Swamiji's idea of salvation, which, in his observation, is a dynamic spiritual process of life.

To develop the spiritual outlook of salvation with social process, Vivekananda interprets two traditional idea of salvation *Jeevan Mukti* or freedom in this life in this world and *Videha Mukti* or the freedom in the life beyond, when there will be the perfect realisation of transcendental value of unity as the non-duality in Absolute or *Brahman*, the substratum of human values. Thus, the idea of *Videha Mukti* makes the idea of *Jivan-Mukti* possible, because it, as the ideal of Transcendental Unity, inspires man to realise this ideal of perfection in this life in different degrees.

Thus, Vivekananda uses the term 'transcendence' in a relative sense as it explains the nature of man as a 'self-transcending being' who tries to transcend his different limitations in different stages of life for a gradual realisation of this value of unity in different states of life and society in different degrees. But as the perfect or total nature of this value is not fully realised in any stage of finite life in this finite world, Vivekananda introduces, the idea of complete realisation of transcendental value of unity as Infinite or Absolute in the life beyond. So the realisation of human value of unity with its manifestations can be explained properly in the background of transcendentality.

But progress of this life towards the life beyond implies the realisation of unity beyond contradictions which we find as continuous and synthetic. This makes the moral and social life of man perfect in different states in different degrees. These states are interrelated and this synthetic and continuous development of human life solves different moral and social problems. The contradiction between the individual and social interest is the fundamental cause of these problems, but the development of unity in man through a selfless process of love and, service, gradually removes these poor contradictions and reconciles them in a harmonious development of the social life of man towards the foundation of unity in society in different degrees. All these degrees of development in different stages of life and society, according to Vivekananda, are the manifestations of perfection or Godness in different forms. This manifestation of Godness in man is nothing but the realisation of potential infiniteness in him that is nothing but the inauguration of God in man.

So this becoming of Man, the God or Man, The Spiritual, through the realisation of perfection in him is the fighting for freedom in unity which is the only truth in Swamiji's Religion of Man. It urges man to realise God through love and service of man as the development of Godness. This is the fundamental idea of Swamiji's *Spiritual Humanism*, when he expresses, "The only God to worship is the human soul in the human body."

In this spiritual process of *Humanism* the emphasis is given on the development of an individual man who is accepted as potentially perfect. But the development of man's life is an evolutionary progress in the manifestation of perfection in life and society in different degrees which becomes complete through a harmonious development of his life with others through which a social unity is established in human life. Thus, in this harmonious development of life, a close relation between man and society is established and in this way the betterment of the life of the individual leads to the betterment of the society. This, in the observation of Vivekananda, is the advancement of human life that becomes complete and perfect through the gradual manifestation of perfection in society.

In this context of the social outlook of *Spiritual Humanism*, the life of Swamiji may also be examined, for his fundamental end in life was the acquirement of salvation for mankind. He got this idea and inspiration for achieving freedom for others, from his master, Sri Ramakrishna who was a great man with several human qualities as discussed in the first part of this book. These human qualities as expression of Godness in Sri Ramakrishna, influenced Vivekananda very much that opened the outer and inner doors for entering into the universality in him, and this urged him to explain and to evaluate the humanitarian and universal outlook of *Indian Spiritualism*. This idea is a synthesis of the absolute spiritual value of unity, supplied by *Vedanta*, and its application in social life on the basis of human outlook supplied by his great master, Sri Ramakrishna. In this background of the synthetic development of *Spiritual humanism*, misunderstanding as held by Professor Adhar Chandra Das requires to be removed. Professor Das pointed out, "...I should like to point out that Swami Vivekananda did not preach Sri Ramakrishna. Instead, he laid emphasis upon *Vedanta,* upon the *Upanisads* as treatises on *Brahman* as impersonal Reality, and as a result he founded Vedanta societies in America and elsewhere."[13]

But it has already been discussed that fundamental end of Swamiji was not to found *Hinduism* on the teachings of *Upanishads* and *Vedanta* but it was to develop the universality in religion as the expression of infiniteness on a synthetic development of the idea of the absolute unity or non-duality as *Advaita,* in its systematic application in human life and society. This is the fundamental end of Vivekananda's religion of man which may also be evaluated as the science of religion as it harmonises the principles of science and religion through the synthesis of the principle of perfection evolved from religion and philosophy and its systematic application in human life through the scientific processes. So, religion, according to Swamiji, is not restriction or imposition, but it is the eternal manifestation and development of perfection in man in society. Thus, it is to be noted in this connection that this religious view of Vivekananda stands on the human outlook as experimented by Sri Ramakrishna in his own existence and that inspires Vivekananda to found a synthetic and democratic outlook of *Humanism* in religion. This idea of religion as introduced by him, is the religion of Man, The Spiritual or the Universal, the Infinite, in man, through the selfless development of life in love and service for mankind, for social justice and equality in a proper development of perfection as unity in men and society.

Notes and References

1. *Complete Works of Swami Vivekananda,* Birth Cent Edn, 1963. Vol I, p. 329.
2. *Ibid,* pp. 331-32.
3. *Complete Works of Swami Vivekananda,* Birth Cent, Edn, 1963,Vol I, p. 17.
4. *Ibid,* p. 19.
5. Practical Vedanta, *Ibid,* Vol. II, p. 293.
6. Vedanta as Privilege, *Ibid,* Vol. I, p. 425.
7. *Ibid,* pp. 422-23.
8. The Vedanta in all its phases, *Ibid,* Vol. III, 1963, p. 341.
9. *Ibid,* Vol II, p. 372
10. *Ibid,* p. 68.
11. *Ibid,* p. 372.
12. R. S. Srivastava, *Contemporary Indian Philosophy,* 1965, pp. 76-77.
13. A. C. Das, *A* Modern *Incarnation* of *God,* 1958, Prefece, p. X.

Part - II

The Philosophy of Spiritual Humanism

Studying the complete works of Swami Vivekananda one can find that experience is a disciplined, a methodical pursuit towards a particular aspect of experience from sciences to religion. The highest goal of man is to realise the interrelated among the different aspects of experiential processes. Speaking in particular of religious experience, Vivekananda says, it is the experience of Divinity in man. This Divinity consciousness is realised by a four-fold discipline of *Jnana* (knowledge), *Karma* (activity-process), *Raja yoga* (disciplined psychology) and *Bhakti* (love and service). This experience being a direct experience resulting out of the above disciplined ways is not abstractly conceptual or empirical. Since behind the conceptual and the perceptual ways, there is a continuous presence of a self-shining experience- which is a resultant process of the above four-fold disciplines- when Vivekananda uses such expressions as universality, unity, oneness, infinity etc. That he refers to is not an abstract conceptual consciousness implied by those words, but their self-shining dynamic experiential process in operation upon the experiential individual and his activity-love and service-to suffering human beings in general belonging to any religion, any state, rich or poor, learned or not learned, man, woman, child and so on or stretching to the animal world or Nature as patterned in its natural condition.

From this comprehensive attitude this chapter has to be shaped and recast through which we find a synthesis of the ideals of *spiritualism* and *humanism*, introducing a new and synthetic outlook of the philosophy of man that develops a practical human outlook in the traditional spiritual ideas of *Upanishads* and *Vedanta*, and also develops a spirit of divinity in the common outlook of *humanism*. In the background of this synthetic outlook, Vivekananda introduces the idea of the religion of man that denies the traditional meaning of religion as the expression of the nature of man who lives in this material world with all material necessities. But the potential perfection as divinity in man makes him a self-transcending being that urges him to transcend the limits of material contradictions for the development of the idea of perfection as unity. This idea of "transcendence" introduces a dynamic change in man for the inauguration of unity in human life, that finally prescribes a change in the social system for the introduction of social unity and equality in and through the awakening of the masses or common men in general.

Through this spiritual and humanistic outlook of the philosophy of religion, Vivekananda thus explains the inner spirit of India, "Here in this blessed land, the foundation and backbone, the life-centre is Religion and Religion alone. Let others talk of politics, of the glory of acquisition of immense wealth poured in by trade, of the power of commercialism, of the glorious fountain of physical liberty…"but India speaks of spiritual freedom in unity in plurality, through the foundation of *Spiritual Socialism* as realised through the four-fold Yogic scheme of *Jnana, Karma, Rajayoga, Bhaktiyoga* as indicated. It is operative with a Divinity in expression in love and service. Vivekananda observes, "So, in India, social reform has to be preached by showing how much more spiritual life the new system will bring and politics has to be preached by showing how much it will improve the one thing that the nation wants its spirituality."[1] In this process of novel *socialism* which is an operative scheme of Divinity in Service and love, Vivekananda applies the ideal of spiritualisation of mankind as a whole in the common life of men in society when "He brings down the Vedanta to fertilise the fields of common life."[2] Thus, through a Spiritual progress in the disciplined aspect as suggested, a man becomes free from *Avidya* or ignorance and the interest for the poor self or ego as the cause of social exploitations, and this progress leads to a perfect and harmonious development of human life in the upliftment of common life through the awakening of all orders of people from "the lower classes are gradually awakening to this fact and making a united front against this, determined to exact their legitimate dues."[3] It is making all self-consciousness in the divine disciplined order. It is not just a conceptual belief in God or a ritualistic or a spiritual God-it is a direct expression of God in one's depth of experiential process.

To discuss the essential characteristics of social exploitation, Vivekananda introduces the method of class analysis on the traditional class or caste system for drawing out the contradiction as the cause of disharmony in society. In "Modern India" he points out that the fundamental basis of the society lies in the progress of the common life of masses or *Shudras*. But the so called upper classes like *Brahmin*, *Kshatriya*, and *Vaishya* in different periods are very busy with their own interests and thus loose the significance of their social outlook as they deprive the common people from their common interest which is the cause of social injustice and inequality. So Vivekananda seeks the harmonious development of society through the development of freedom in unity as can be enjoyed and shared by all by the contributions of four-fold process of acquisition through the expression of Divinity in love and service. He writes, "...a time will come when there will be the rising of the *Shudra* class, with their *Shudra-hood*; that is to say, not like that as at present, when the *Shudras* are becoming great by acquiring the characteristic; qualities of the *Vaishya* or the *Kshatriya*, but a time will come, when the *Shudras* of every country, with their inborn *Shudra* nature and habits, not becoming in essence *Vaishya* or *Kshatriya*, but remaining as *Shudras* will gain absolute supremacy in every society."[4] This is the neo-communistic outlook of Swamiji, that does not ignore any element in man, but on the other hand, he wants to establish *Shudras* with the *development* of Shudra element in its harmony with other elements in men. This is possible, as already mentioned, through the prescription of the practice of the four-fold Yogic process towards transcendent divinity through service and love; which is a freedom in expression of in a transformed social milieu. This outlook of Swami Vivekananda, according to Chelishev, is revolutionary which is evaluated by him in the following way- "It seems to us that when

Vivekananda spoke of a radical reform he meant a revolutionary change in the social system, in other words, for his views Vivekananda understood the active role of the masses in the historical development of his country. This is shown in particular by his statement that the influence and power of the *Kshatriya* and the wealth of the *Vaishya* are possible only thanks to the physical work of *Shudra*. It is they that form the true body of any society."[5]

Here we find the similarity of the idea of Vivekananda with the view of Karl Marx, the founder of the philosophy of *Communism*. Vivekananda, like Marx, wants the awakening of *Shudras* like the upliftment of proletariat by Marx. Both of them introduce the method of class analysis of man for explaining the contradictions in society and thus they desire to establish man in society removing all types of alienations. Be it noted whereas Karl Marx's approach to society is socio-political, Vivekananda's approach is broadly humanist from his transformed disciplined religious perspective as indicated.

Thus, the new outlook of *Humanism*, introduced by Vivekananda which is from a disciplined religious perspective is different from Karl Marx's standpoint which is restricted to economic-political sphere of existence. According to these thinkers, man is the centre of history and essence of man lies in his freedom, but freedom has to be interpreted as a pervasive process behind all orders of experience. Following Vedanta, Vivekananda explains the freedom of man as his essential features for the manifestation of the consciousness of unity in Him. Here the unity as suggested is a special unity as related to a discipline which is universal hence divine. But Marx takes man as the evolution of matter where consciousness is evolved from the complex organisation of matter. Through the development of this consciousness, a man becomes free from all types of exploitations, and tries to engage himself to be a free man." Man, in this process of achieving freedom from exploitations, express his "productive being" as a creative potentiality, which, in his observation, is the real nature of man as "Productive powers", "Productive forces", "Vital" and "Essential powers". Then in *Early Writings* Marx points out that the history of man, is the "External unfolding of human essential powers: ..." and in this way he observes that "...the nature that develops in human history and in the history of industrial progress is the real nature of man".

Though the essential human nature, in the observation of Marx, is evolved through the material process of evolution from a preceding animal species in a Darwinian form, the creative potency or the real nature of man makes him qualitatively different from animal. For this man like animal, may work for the satisfaction of his primary instinctive needs, yet unlike animal, he works freely for the expression or the realisation of the real human nature that makes him a true human being.

According to Marx, the essential human nature as the infinite power in man, makes him a real Man over animal, that inspires him to work freely for fighting against exploitation as the cause of his alienation in the capitalistic form of society. In *Economic and Political Manuscripts,* Marx explains accordingly this state as a state of dehumanisation where a man, "...No longer feels himself to he anything but an animal", and this, in his observation, is due to socio-economic exploitation in four forms as self alienation from the process of that work, alienation from the products of labour, alienation of the worker from himself and alienation of the worker from others."[7] Thus, in the capitalist system the classes, division of labour and money are mainly responsible for alienation of human beings, because under these processes man are treated as commodities.

In "Early Writings," Marx again points out, "The worker becomes an ever cheaper commodity. The devaluation of the human world increases in direct relation with the increase in value of the world of things".

Thus, making of man a "cheaper commodity" related to the "devaluation of the human world", according to Marx, is the alienation of man from his essential nature that is due to different types of socio-economic exploitations. For this Marx wants the socio-economic change through the introduction of *Communism* as the philosophy of scientific socialism on social and equal sharing of private properties or entire wealth.

Like Karl Marx, Vivekananda also is seriously concerned with this problem of alienation of man. According to Marx, it is due to economic exploitations and Vivekananda, also like him, explains the socio-economic exploitations of man as leading to the growth of different classes in society and is fully aware of the alienated conditions of life of the poor classes or masses as "*Shudra*" in India. He observes, "The poor, the low, the sinners in India have no friends; no help-they cannot rise, try however they may. They sink lower and lower every day, they feel the blows showered upon them by a cruel society, and they do not know when the blow comes. They have forgotten they are men."[8]

He evaluates that the cause of the downfall of India as a nation, to be due to alienated condition of labour classes or common masses, who according to Vivekananda, are its real citizens and so he, like Marx, also wants the change of socio-economic system through which common people may be free from exploitation and thus can acquire their lost individualities with the proper realisation of real human nature. So he welcomes the rising of *Shudra* class, and also observes, "...the times have changed. The lower classes are gradually awakening to this fact and making a united front against this, determined to exact their legitimate dues."[10]

In this connection it may also be pointed out that with the change of socio-economic orders, through the awakening of common men, Vivekananda does not want to denounce other properties or human qualities, present in other classes of people. He, on the other hand, wants the harmonious development of human personality for the realisation of the total nature of man as the true individuality, which, in the observation of Vivekananda, helps him to overcome the self-alienation as the negation of any element of human existence. So, in this process, Vivekananda, like Marx, though accepts economic exploitation as a cause of inequality, being responsible for alienation, still to him it is only an one-sided interpretation. His deliberation, in this context, as a comprehensive and disciplined form is a creative and synthetic programme, where all aspects of experience are coherently related to the expression of the perfect nature of man in a humanistic process. In this way Vivekananda observes that the urge for the enjoyment of a particular privilege in the society, expressing particular property as power, compels a man to exploit others physically, mentally, and even spiritually, Firstly, man tries to satisfy his physical or animal needs through which a strongman exploits the weak on the basis of physical ability and economic stability. Then an intelligent man, through his intellectual superiority tries to control others, and lastly, a man, through a spiritual knowledge regarding religion, God etc. can also exploit others. For this, Marx rejected religion as the opium for the exploitation of the people. Vivekananda points out that the misuse of these abilities or powers leads to the growth of the complexity in different classes e.g. *Brahmin, Kshatriya, Vaishya, Shudra* and men of these different classes through their particular abilities try to ignore other abilities of men and thus obstruct the development of different qualities of people. But in this connection Vivekananda observes that through the enjoyment of a particular privilege a man of particular class may misuse his power and so comes in confrontation with others, which, according to Marx may be called as 'class-struggle'. In this process, as Vivekananda observes, a particular class looses its power and in this way there will be a change of power in the society. He explains that in the age of *Brahmin* an emphasis was given on the birth right to the intellectual superiority of man that forced him to dominate others. In the age of *Kshatriya*, the physical power of men of a particular class was very much important that made them strong to exploit the weak physically: Then comes the age of *Vaishya*, or the age of capitalists when economic power is centred to a particular class of people, who are exploiting the common men both physically and economically, which, according to both Vivekananda and Marx, are responsible for the alienation of man in modern society. But Vivekananda points out that there again will be a change of power with the rise of the age of *Shudras* through the awakening of proletariat or poor people. For this uprising of the *Shudra* power properly, Vivekananda prescribes an over-all discipline of his four-fold disciplines to realise a comprehensive process and activity. Vivekananda evaluates the social and practical implication of this process in the following manner, "Each soul is potentially divine. The goal (of life) is to manifest this divinity within, by controlling nature, external (by science, technology, and socio-political process) and internal (by ethics and religion). Do this either by work or worship or psychic control or philosophy, by one or all of these and BE FREE. This is the whole of religion. Doctrines or dogmas or rituals or temples or forms are secondary details"[11]

But if we put an emphasis on the development of mere economic and physical ability, ignoring the synthetic process of developing other qualities of man as the expression of total or divine nature of man, then in the age of *Shudra* management Swamiji warns, "...There will be the extension of happiness and physical prosperity, but the weakness of this age is that there may he degradation of civilisation. The scope of common education may be wider, but there will be a gradual decrease of the man of extraordinary genius."[12] The reference is here to the qualitative perfection of man which cannot be short of disciplined Divinity with service and love, as already pointed out. This, according to Vivekananda, is for the real freedom from alienation which, in his observation, is not external but internal as the alienation from divine nature of man. External security cannot always solve this problem of alienation, which, as Vivekananda observes, is internal in nature. For this he puts an importance on developing the total individuality as the expression of both external and internal nature of men.

So, for the proper development of human life and for the establishment of man in a qualitatively perfect order of society, when Marx introduces *Communism* as the transcendence of private property for the real appropriation of the human essence, Vivekananda thinks about the introduction of the ideal state for the harmonious development of the human essence, where "...there will be an equilibrium of the element of knowledge of the age of Brahmin, civility of *Kshatriya*, self-developing power of Vaishya and Sudra's ideal of equality, but there will be the absence of their disadvantages that will lead to the formation of an ideal state."[13] This is a social process of balanced disciplined principles exhibited in Swamiji's four-fold prusuit towards Divinity, Service and Love.

The foundation of this ideal state as focused by Vivekananda, is the essential part of the harmonious development of human life and society. Before this stage is finally realised often there is an interplay of two conditioning powers - one creates difference, the other unity. Swamiji observes, "In the formation of social life there are the superiorities of two powers - one is creating difference and other is establishing unity. These take different forms in different names in different countries in different times....The whole universe is the playground of unity in plurality and plurality in unity; the world is a play of equality and differences."[14] Vivekananda points out that the fundamental end of social life is to develop unity in and through the differences. So according to him, "Fundamental work is to proceed towards equality and unity, not through the elimination of plurality."[15]

In the development of this new democratic outlook, Vivekananda ignores the process of elimination that leads to the origin of particular class, but on the other hand he puts an emphasis on the harmonious development of human personality in and through the differences. So Vivekananda's idea of state is not the surrender of men to it, but state as the collection of different human beings, standing on the harmonious development of human personalities towards integral process, where there is a role of the four-fold yogic disciplines.

Thus, the introduction of this new order of humanistic outlook in the social, political and other orders in general including religious order, is the fundamental end of Vivekananda, when he puts an importance on the essential development of human nature as the natural expression of man as the religion of man. For in this process, Vivekananda explains the essential feature of religion and practical and spiritual implication of *Vedanta* as *Practical Vedanta* which is for the development of new order of *Spiritual Humanism*. This idea changes the anti-humanistic attitude of religion that according to Marx, is "illusory sun which revolves round man." It, on the other hand, develops the humanistic outlook of religion and philosophy that urges man to revolve round himself and thus inspires him to know, the significance of his material and social existences in and through the harmonious development of his infinite personality or potential perfection towards the manifestation of unity in life in different degrees, expressing the divinity in life and society, which in the observation of Vivekananda, is socio-spiritual in nature. So, this process, according to him, is the transcendence of external and internal contradictions as the causes of self-alienation, and also is the introduction of unity in differences or contradictions for reconciliation as humanisation. In the interpretation of this programme, Vivekananda argues that man will be *Vedantist* and will demand any special privilege in physical or intellectual or spiritual in form, is self-contradictory. Because *Vedanta* observes infinite power or potency in all creatures which is manifested in them in different degrees. In this background, Vivekananda points out that in a proper situation a worm can also develop human value. So in this expanded process of unity and universality, the humanistic programme of overcoming limitations or contradictions, becomes the proper foundation of *Practical Vedanta* or religion of human life and existence. For this Vivekananda declares, 'Our ideal is the *Brahman* of spiritual culture and renunciation'.

This ideal for *Brahman* as Oneness or Unity, according to Vivekananda, is the basis of 'Spiritual culture' as the intercultural process of developing harmony in the humanistic way of 'renunciation' of differences or contradictions.

It expresses the inner significance of *Spiritual Humanism* which can also be realised and can also be applied on human life and society through the introduction of human or social ideals of selfless love and unconditional service for mankind. So the *Humanism* of Vivekananda includes both the human ideal of perfection in man as an end and the human process of realisation of this ideal as the means, through which this ideal can be manifested in human life.

Thus, Vivekananda's idea of *Spiritual Humanism*, developed through the selfless love and service for mankind makes him prominent in contemporary Indian philosophy and relates him intimately with the inner and eternal spirit of India. In this connection, it may be said that Vivekananda, like all other contemporary Indian thinkers, tries to explain and evaluate the traditional Indian thinking of *Vedas* and *Upanishads*, other systems of Indian Philosophy, different systems of Religion and Culture etc. and through this evaluation on a comparative study of the East and the West, he develops this new form of *Humanism* as the religion of humanity in an intercultural context, where the inauguration of Divinity in man as Man, The Spiritual in and through disciplined process, is very much important.

In order to explain the significance of *Humanism*, as developed by Swami Vivekananda, we may refer to a brief history of expanding *Humanism* in West with its limitation. In this connection it may be pointed out that Western *Humanism* is closely related to the humanistic idea developed by Greeks, Romans and Christians. The two non-religious forms of Greek and Roman *Humanism* were restricted to purely Greeks or to Romans only and the religious form of Christian *Humanism*, though related to the general people of Europe, was very much limited by narrow theological creeds and dogmas. Due to these limitations and restrictions, these forms of *Humanism* paved the way for Thirty-Years War between Protestants and Catholics in Germany, when one killed others in the name of God. This sad experience of war compelled the people of Europe to seek man in this worldly state of materialistic development in science and culture, instead of God as other worldly state of being. But both the first world war and the second world war destroyed the total faith of people of the West, either in man or in God as human and superhuman values.

In this situation, a new hope from the USSR, in the form of Bolshevik Revolution, leading to the development of Marxian outlook of *Humanism*, created the socio-economic change for the awakening of common men or masses. In this connection we may also refer to the awakening of the 18th century in Europe, which was recognised by Russell as "Romantic Movement" as "...a profound revolt both philosophical and political, against traditional systems in thought."[15] The inner spirit of this revolution was to evaluate the creative states of man as the expressions of goodness in him.

This wave of the revolutionary spirit of the West for the cultivation of the collective life through the awakening of the common people with the expression of collective goodness as the manifestation of infinite potency as creative greatness in man brought a Renaissance in Bengal and in other parts of India. This created a creative humanistic outlook that inspired different thinkers in India to evaluate the humanistic thought of India in the background of revolutionary humanistic process of the West. It also got a creative inspiration under the influence of Sri Ramakrishna and Vivekananda and thus paved the way for developing human outlook in a more creative form. This type of creative outlook of man is also developed by other contemporary Indian thinkers like Rabindranath, Sri Aurobindo and Mahatma Gandhi. R. Rolland rightly points out "the present leaders of India, the King of thinkers, the King of poets, and the Mahatma Aurobindo Ghosh, Tagore and Gandhi-have grown, flowered, and borne fruit under the double constellation of the Swan and the Eagle-a fact publicly acknowledged by Aurobindo and Gandhi."[16]

The Renaissance of Nineteenth Century in India, emerging from these great thinkers, was nothing but the awakening of man. This, according to Vivekananda, is the establishment of man to a higher order of human perfection, which is the four-fold disciplined processes of *Jnana-Karma-Raja* and *Bhakti.* Inspired by this disciplined ways, Vivekananda says, "...may I be born again and again and suffer thousands of miseries so that I may worship the only God, that exists, the only god I believe in, the sum total of all souls and above all my God the wicked, my God the miserable, my God the poor of all races, of all species, is the special object of my worship."[17]

Here lies the uniqueness of Vivekananda's interpretation of the philosophy of man that is creative and synthetic and thus is spiritual. Vivekananda, in this connection, explains the creative states of individual and his collective or social existence in the background of the synthetic development of this idea of Divinity as the introduction of unity in life and existence in different degrees. This, in the observation of Vivekananda, is Union or *Yoga* that is a spiritual process as the transcendence of limitations or contradictions on one hand and the inauguration of Unity as Divinised Humanity or Godness in man on the other. Vivekananda's approach to philosophical or religious experience through his four-fold *Yoga* to Divinity as love and service to humanity, according to R. Rolland, is the creative expression of social equality and justice. Here his emphasis is on unity in the process of love and service, and therein lies a common awakening of all to a perfect condition, Western and Eastern. It is also expressed in other Indians of his time- in Raja Rammohan Roy, Vidyasagar, Bankim Chandra and Madhusudan. They were all inspired by their mother country, having the consciousness of the awakening western reforming ideas of their times.

In the words of R. Rolland, the idea of unity, as traditional and prospective programme, may be evaluated thus, "Unity of every Indian man and woman (and world-unity as well); of all the powers of the spirit, dream and action; reason, love and work. Unity of the hundred races of India with their hundred different tongues and hundred thousand gods springing from the same religious centre, the core of present and future reconstruction. Unity of thousand sects of *Hinduism*. Unity within the vast ocean of all religious thought and all rivers past and present, Western and Eastern. For, and here in lies the difference "between the awakening of Sri Ramakrishna and Vivekananda and that of Rammohan Roy and the Brahmo Samaj- in these days India refuses allegiance to the imperious civilisation of the West, she defends her own ideas; she has stepped into her age-long heritage with the firm intention not to sacrifice any part of it, but to allow the rest of the world to profit by it, and to receive in return the intellectual conquests of the West."[18]

In the background of this evaluation, if the significance of the idea of unity in thought and activities of different contemporary thinkers of Bengal are examined, it is found that in Rammohan Roy, its realisation can be possible through the development of reason or intellect, in Vidyasagar, Madhusudan and others, it can be realised through the development of emotion or heart, in Bankim Chandra and others we find the interrelation of intellect and emotion but finally in Vivekananda the spiritual significance of the ideal of unity is found where there is a synthesis of intellect or knowledge, emotion or love, action or service in the eternal spirit of man as Man, The Spiritual. This synthetic outlook of Swamiji, as developed in the idea of Man, The Spiritual, according to Dr Govinda Chandra Dev, makes him "...a great advocate of equilibrium between warring forces of life: reason and faith, matter and spirit, individual and society, Science and religion, the past and the present, the East and the West and last but not the least, haves and have notes." Here lies the human and social significance or the idea of unity through the development of synthetic outlook in man and society and again it is also spiritual as it lies in the manifestation of Divinity as transcendental prospect in different degrees. For this Swamiji observes, "Religion is neither word nor doctrine. It is to be and become...", that leads to the development of spirituality as "Universal Man" in individual man, which is explained by R. Rolland as "...Universal soul was rooted in its human soul" in the millieu of differences, in outlook and attitudes.

This explains the inner significance of *Spiritual Humanism*, as developed by Swami Vivekananda. This type of the philosophy of man as ideal and as a process, is evaluated by Swami Ranganathananda, "This is humanism with the deepest spiritual import and, therefore, with the widest social relevance, most stable and steady and therefore, beyond the reach of the pressures, narrow and violent, of all political, racial, and religious prejudices, frenzies and passions."[19]

Regarding the development of this philosophy as the expression of the consciousness of universality by a contrast, as discovered in man, Vivekananda's idea maybe compared to other contemporary Indian thinkers, like Rabindranath, Gandhi and Sri Aurobindo, as all of them follow the traditional Indian outlook of *Vedas* and *Upanishads* and accept man as "potentially Divine" and also recognise the need of a disciplined process of love and service for the realisation of Divinity in man. In this process, all of them put an emphasis on education or social training, and so "Sri Ramakrishna Mission", the revolutionary organisation in spirit and activities, was established by Swami Vivekananda. This type of revolutionary outlook also was developed through equally novel and powerful organisations like Visva-Bharati at Santiniketan, founded by Rabindranath, Sabarmati Asrama of Gandhiji, and Sri Aurobindo Asrama at Pondicherry. They may be regarded as organised programme for bringing a social change of India in the milieu of advancing world process to progressive civilised orders of the world at large.

But if the views of all these thinkers are carefully examined it is found that both Vivekananda and Sri Aurobindo pay a special stress on the spiritual process and so they emphasise the *Yoga* as a transcendent-experiential process, but Rabindranath and Gandhi put an importance on the moral and cultural process of life. For this both Gandhi and Tagore observe the ultimate Reality as truth and love.

In *Young India* Gandhi identifies God with truth and love. The realisation of God as truth in human life, according to him, is the "obedience to the moral law", which, in his observation, is the extension of human relation as the development of godness in man through the human is process of disinterested love and service to humanity. Rabindranath also emphasises the social development of the cultural relation of man through the human process of love and social service, and so he avoids the imposition of compulsion on the seekers of truth in his curriculum of Visva Bharati. He articulates its objectives as "to bring into more intimate relation with one another, through patient study and research, the different cultures of the East on the basis of their underlying unity to approach the west from the stand point of such a unity of the life and thought of Asia and to seek to realise in a common fellowship of study the meeting of the East and West, and thus ultimately to strengthen the fundamental conditions of world peace of through the establishment of free communication of ideas between the two of hemispheres." So the development of the cultural relation of unity among men through a socio-cultural development, is the fundamental object of Rabindranath; but the final end of Vivekananda is to establish the spiritual brotherhood through the spiritual development of man in a spiritual process of *Yoga* in love and service to mankind. The significance of this spiritual outlook of Swami Vivekananda is evaluated by Swami Ranganathananda, thus, "He accepts the human situation, man as we find him in society. He also accepts the need for the manipulation of his socio-political conditions, upto a point, to ensure his growth and development. But he will insist that man must develop and grow further, that he must evolve and steadily unfold also the higher divine possibilities hidden within him."[20]

Thus, it is to be noted in this connection that both Tagore and Gandhi put a special emphasis on the humanistic approach to Reality as Reality is taken by them as the substratum of human value of love and thus can be realised through disinterested service of mankind. But this Reality is also taken by Vivekananda and Sri Aurobindo as love, but they explain this love as power which is to be developed spiritually, through the transcendent-experiential process of *Yoga*.

For this, to Sri Aurobindo, Reality is *Sakti* or *dynamic Divine* which has two forms - cosmic and transcendent.

The cosmic process is related to the problems of present circumstances and the transcendent process is the transcendent-experiential programme through yoga for the divine descent in man for changing man to Superman with the total development of "powers into the Divine". The realisation of this Divine power or Transcendent Divine, according to Sri Aurobindo, is the final salvation of man, which, he observes, can be possible through meditation in a supramoral and supra-mental plan. Regarding the cultivation of the uniqueness of this spirit and process of meditation, Sri Aurobindo points out, "For myself it was Sri Ramakrishna who personally came and first turned me to this Yoga. Vivekananda in the Alipore Jail gave me the foundations of that knowledge which is the basis of our Sadhana."[21]

But, in this connection it should be mentioned here that though Sri Aurobindo is influenced by Vivekananda in his transcendental meditation and though he puts an emphasis on the spiritual development of human life, Vivekananda's *spiritualism* does not stand on supra-moral and supra-mental plan of Sri Aurobindo. His *spiritualism* is the extension of *Universalism* in the development of Divine Unity in man through *yoga* as a socio-moral process of selfless love and unconditional service for mankind. In this way his philosophy of religion expresses the philosophy of the of man as the religion of man which is not the imposition of any idea of Divinity on man but is a natural expression of Divinity in man through socio-moral process. E.N. Komarov evaluates this process, "...religion is in him a theory and practice of its own kind of moral perfection. If he regarded the concept as 'attainment of God' or 'religious realisation' (realisation of God) as the essence and meaning of religion, then moral perfection precisely was virtually the main content of the very concept of 'realisation'. In this context Vivekananda interpreted the positions of Hindu religious-philosophical system of *Vedanta*, stating that it revealed the secret of 'selfless work.'"[22] So all these thinkers lay a especial stress on the humanistic development of life in society. Rabindranath and Gandhi think about this development of the cultural relation of man on a socio-moral plan and so *Humanism*, introduced by these thinkers may be called *Cultural Humanism*. But as Swamiji and Sri Aurobindo emphasise the spiritual development of man as the synthetic expression of socio-spiritual existence, their *Humanism* is called *Spiritual Humanism*.

If the character of Swamiji's *Spiritual Humanism* is properly evaluated, it is found that it may be transcendental in nature. Because as *Humanism* is spiritual, the human values in the spiritual programme are to be realised in human life in different stages in different degrees. Still it must be noted that Vivekananda puts an especial emphasis on the practical application of this transcendental or spiritual value in social and human life through a practical and socio-moral process of love and service of mankind. These methods of disinterested love and service for man make the highest ideal of truth to be practically applicable to the society that make the society as ideal and real. For this Swamiji rightly observes, "That society is the greatest, where the highest truths become practical. That is my opinion; and if society is not fit for the highest truths, make it so, and the sooner, the better."[23] This outlook of practical and social approach to truth as transcendental ideal, is evaluated by E. Chelishev thus, "In his desire to elevate man, Vivekananda puts forward the idea that the higher divine substance–*Brahman*-is personified in millions of ordinary living people and therefore the worship of God is tantamount to serving man. He called for the all round development of human personality and the assertion of man's right to happiness in this world and the fostering in the ordinary man of a sense of his own dignity."[24]

Thus, it may be said that the fundamental basis of the human outlook of Swamiji as love for man is "the fostering in the ordinary man of a sense of his own dignity," as observed by E. Chelishev. This idea of Vivekananda with humanistic programme, makes him close to Buddha, a noted Humanist of the East and other Humanists of the West though they have differences from each other. Both Vivekananda and Gautama Buddha are to be recognised as Humanists, as both of them think about the sorrows and the sufferings of common men and try to introduce the human ideals of love and service for the removal of these contradictions. But the fundamental end of the *Spiritual*

Humanism of Vivekananda is the spiritual freedom of men that stands on *Atmatattva* or the realisation of own self in everything. On the other hand, the end of Buddha's *Humanism* is to acquire "*Nirvana*," that stands on the theory of Not-self or *Nairtmavada.* So Buddha does not believe in the self and the freedom of the self and puts an emphasis on the freedom of man in society through the introduction of socio-moral relation in men that ignores the transcendental aspect of reality. Radhakrishnan points out that the development of this moral outlook of Buddha is to "set aside the transcendental aspect as being indemonstrable to thought and unnecessary to morals, and emphasise the ethical universalism of the Upanisads."[25]

So it may be pointed out that in order to develop the neo-humanistic outlook, Buddha ignored the Upanishadic transcendentality but emphasised the "the ethical universalism of Upanishads." In *Patravalee* (Vol. I) Vivekananda evaluated this programme of *Nirvana* "...in his unrivalled sympathy." This sympathy of Buddha, is for all men, overcoming all types of sufferings and miseries, which may be examined by Chatterjee thus, "...the object of nirvana is not to put an end to one's own misery, but to obtain perfect wisdom with which the liberated can try for the salvation of all being in misery. It also believes that Buddha's watchful eyes are on all miserable beings and that through his mercy and help they will be liberated."[26] It is a continuous social process that proves the right of acquiring liberation or *Nirvana,* by all sections of people. This, in the opinion of Buddha, can be possible by right actions for others, which in the observation of Sarkar, "...can be operative in the true spirit of the six paramitas or perfections. These are processes of (i) Dana (giving), (ii) Sila (observing the precepts), (iii) Virya (spirit of manhood), (iv) Ksanti (humility or practice), (v) Dhyana (Meditation) and Prajna (transcendental wisdom). The Buddhist life begins with giving and ends with transcendental wisdom (prajna)."[27] The 'transcendental wisdom' contains the idea of liberation in this life or the life beyond, through a continuous humanistic process, related to a chain of cause and effect in birth and rebirth. So in this programme, though Buddha does not believe in immortal, permanent or unchanging process of self, he admits the unbroken continuity of human consciousness. This is evaluated by Chatterjee, "Man's life is a unbroken series of states which are causally connected, just a lamp burning all day and night is an unbroken series of different flames which are causally connected. Again, as from one lamp another may be lighted, and though the two are different, they are connected causally; similarly, the end-state of this life may cause the beginning of the next. Therefore, rebirth is not transmigration, i.e. migration of the same soul into another body; it is the causation of the next life by the present. The conception of a permanent soul is thus replaced here by that of an unbroken stream of consciousness as in the philosophy of David Hume and of William James."[28]

In the context of this analysis, the humanistic process of liberation, as advanced by Buddha as "an unbroken stream of consciousness", is closely associated with the socio-moral or spiritual awakening of humanity as the proper inauguration of unity in men and society. This idea of unity of practical socio-normal programme of love and service, as examined by Buddha, with the advancement of the spiritual process of human unity and social harmony, as conceptually evaluated by *Upanishads* and *Vedanta* that develop a proper spirit of unity in the creative humanistic outlook of Vivekananda. This is evaluated by Gobinda Chandra Dev, "The long and short of it all is that Buddha is not prepared to make room for a philosophy of unity in his code of morality. But his unqualified emphasis on service to man, more precisely to all living beings, his prayer for their welfare: *"Sabbe Satta sukhita hantu"*–"let all living beings be happy", is logically quite consistent and compatible with the notion of unity in *vedanta* of which Vivekananda is the most eloquent exponent of our times."[29]

In the background of this humanistic analysis of creative unity, Vivekananda finally emphasises the universalism of *Upanishads* and *Vedanta* on the basis of the realisation of the universal existence of Self in man as universal unity with all and is finally identical with God or Absolute–'*Ayamatma Brahma*'. Thus, Swamiji's idea of *Humanism* stands on the spiritual outlook of '*Atmatattva*' or '*Brhamaattva*' that takes Man or self or God as identical. So, this outlook of Swamiji introduces the idea of Divinity in Man as Man, The Spiritual through a humanistic process of love for man as "to love man is to serve God."

Swamiji observes that God as spiritual ideal is manifested in human life as human value and a man, through the realisation of this spiritual value in humanistic process, also becomes spiritual or divine. Swamiji points out that it is the only way of man of becoming great and for this he emphasises, "Faith, faith, faith in ourselves, faith in God- this is the secret of greatness." This faith in man about the faith in greatness in man may be called the divinity in him, which is explained by Vivekananda as "That faith calls out the divinity within." This faith in man inspires him to accept a man among all his contradictions like sorrows and sufferings, that finally helps him to love man as God, which is the only method of man of becoming God or Divine.

In the background of this idea of divinisation of man, it may be noted that the fundamental object of Swamiji's *Spiritual Humanism*, is to develop the potential divinity in man expressing his multi-dimensional nature; which is absent in the interpretation of the term *Humanism*, supplied by Western humanists.

Comte, the renowned positivist, denies the term Divinity as it is used in religion and philosophy. He points out that the first stage of human civilisation was the age of religion when one type of fetishism was accepted through the imposition of godness in nature and material object. Then came the age of philosophy and lastly through the development of positive philosophy in the Nineteenth Century, man, through the development of his scientific knowledge, learns to deny the imposition of Godness in nature and material object and finally observes that the centre of this world is man. Regarding the nature and development of the concept of man in positive philosophy of Comte. Dr Bandyopadhyay points out, "his only controller is neither God nor Philosophy, but is his own self-determination, acquired through knowledge and science."[30]

Materialism and Marxism also put an importance on man on his material progress, and so deny his divinity. But as these thoughts ignore the idea of freedom as the free and independent development of human existence, and as these thoughts put also much emphasis upon the material and social determinations, the humanistic outlook of the philosophy of *Existentialim* arises as the reaction of this deterministic thinking, and it accepts the independent existence of man with his freedom. But Existentialists also do not put any importance on the idea of divinity as the expression of greatness as perfection in man. So *Existentialism*, like *Positivism*, has no faith in divinity and thus do not believe in achieving perfection as the development of human values. For this the humanistic idea of existential philosophy is evaluated thus: "With its emphasis on individuality, existentialism is undoubtedly a predominantly liberal-philosophy, but it is a liberalism with no belief in a natural social harmony and no hope in man's perfectibility."[31] So it may be said that this liberal thinking, though puts an importance on the independent existence of man, this humanistic approach to human life deals with only a limited and a particular aspect of man which fails to explain the total potentialities of man, developing perfect unity.

In the context of this analysis of human existence and freedom, it may also be pointed out that different thinkers, in different ages, have tried to interpret the term man in different senses from different perspectives, that, in the first stage of the analysis of man, have created two extreme views- *Naturalism*, and *Absolutism*. Both these views ignore the independent and free existence of man as unique personality. *Naturalism* includes man under nature and so treats man as natural phenomenon, and *Absolutism* also accepts the existence of Absolute idea over man and thus denies his freedom.

Then with a change in the naturalistic and absolutistic explanations of man, the *neo-naturalism* and the idea of concrete universal, introduced in modern *Absolutism*, accept the free development of human life and existence. This finally lead to the development of a modern and liberal outlook of man, dealing with his free and independent existence. As it is concerned with the uniqueness of human freedom, so this idea is named as *Humanism*. In *Humanism,* F.C.S. Schiller explains this liberal idea in philosophy stands against the restricted views of *Naturalism* and *Absolutism*. *Humanism*, on the other hand, cultivates the philosophic attitude which accepts the analysis of human experience as the primary basis of all philosophical explanations.

But in this liberal humanistic approach, we may also find the explanation of man in a limited sense where he is taken as the finite man that puts an emphasis on the limited material aspect as material '*ego*' of man and thus makes man as limited as anthropocentric, which, according to Maritain, is 'in-human humanism.'

For this, there arises wider interpretation of *Humanism* as *Divine Humanism*, dealing with infinite potentiality and creative intercultural possibility of man as developing his unique and infinite personality. This view of *Humanism* puts an importance on the development of the potential infiniteness of man that makes him great. In *True Humanism,* J. Maritain evaluates this greatness thus, ".....man more truly human and to make his original greatness manifest by causing him to participate in all that can enrich him in nature in history."

In the background of this humanistic analysis of the "original greatness" of man, Swami Vivekananda, like some Western humanists of his time, also puts importance on this creative greatness, expressed through man's intellectual, social, cultural and spiritual attainments. Swamiji, in his new outlook of *Spiritual Humanism* as the proper development of the religion of humanity, emphasises the socio-spiritual programme for the realisation of the divinity in man as the Man, The Spiritual with the realisation and expression of innumerable social and spiritual values, making him more divine and great.

Thus, in this context of the evaluation of the idea of Man, The Spiritual as the expression of spiritual or transcendental values with different social and human qualities, developing humanity as the manifestation of creative greatness of man in different states of existence, it may be noted that the fundamental object of Swamiji's religion of man is to found the philosophy of the *Spiritual Humanism*. It places man as Spiritual or Divine or Great. Vivekananda examines this process in a socio-spiritual way. As man exists in this material world he must have material demands which cannot be ignored. But satisfaction of mere individual interest or narrow material demands of life makes a man more limited and selfish. But his social nature as potential greatness, directs him to think about his collective existence in the wider social life that inspires him to work for social interest and to think about the large and collective life, as the centre of his collective or social existence. This spirit in man urges him finally to work for others beyond his ownself and other limitation of interests that relates him to others, expressing disinterested feeling in love for the development of unity with all.

In this way, Swamiji observes that Man, in this human and social process of life and activities, can overcome his material limitations and contradictions and can gradually realise the infinite personality as creative greatness through a proper realisation of divinity as unity in men and society. This can be possible through the socio-spiritual process of *yoga* in its humanistic approach to love and service for others. This, according to Swamiji, is humanistic and social process, but it is spiritual or transcendental in nature as there are degrees of realisations of these values in human life and society in different stages is through the degrees of manifestations in love and service in different states of mankind in harmony.

Thus, in developing the programme of the religion of man as the expression of creative greatness or multi-dimensional divinity, Vivekananda examines his philosophy of Man, The Spiritual as the process of founding *Humanism* as *Spiritual Humanism*.

In Western *Humanism*, there is a faith in the greatness of man as expressed through his different socio-cultural activities in this material world. But there are unlimited creative possibilities in man, beyond this limited humanistic analysis. For this Vivekananda explains this creativity as the potential infiniteness or divinity in man as Man, The Spiritual. This idea of man does not merely explain the material or individual existence of man with the material development of life. But it, on the other hand, synthesises the materiality with the spirituality and thus evaluates the material or individual, collective or social and spiritual or transcendental values of life with their expressions in harmonious forms and manners. In order to explain the infinite potency of man, Vivekananda points out, "Do you know how much energy, how many powers, how many forces, are still lurking behind that frame of yours? What scientist has known all that is in man? Millions of years have passed since man first came here, and yet but-one infinitesimal part of his powers has been manifested. Therefore, you must not say that you are weak. How do you know that possibilities lie behind that degradation on the surface? You know but little of that which is within you. For behind you is the ocean of infinite power and blessedness."[32] In this way Vivekananda pleads for Man, The Spiritual, expressing the creative multinatured divinity as "the ocean of infinite power and blessdeness." Man, in the observation of Vivekananda, has an unlimited fund of energy which is not fully exhausted in fulfilling his limited material or biological demands. But unlimited energy in man, expressed through the different creative states of existence, develop his infinite personality as the manifestation of his potential perfection as the sense of unity.

So the process of developing Man, The Spiritual of Infinite in man, the individual, according to Vivekananda, is a dynamic and harmonious development of human existence overcoming limitations and self-contradictions through disinterested human ideals of love and service for men, with the advancement of the humanistic relation of unity in individual, social and universal states of existence.

This humanistic programme of Vivekananda, on one hand supplies the rational account of the human ideals of love and social service with their harmonious expressions in life and existence and on the other hand, evaluates the ontological status of man in the development of socio-spiritual relation of unity. This idea of man in the development of the philosophy of *Humanism*, is examined by Varma thus, "Humanism seeks the expansion of the range of awareness for the appreciation of the frontiers of the multi-dimensional man. This can be possible either through the disinterested action or through the philosophic and scientific contemplation."[33]

Thus, in the background of this evaluation of the ideas of Man and *Humanism* in the form of *Spiritual Humanism*, advanced by Swami Vivekananda, we get a synthetic analysis of "multidimensional man" in a spiritual process of developing individuality and universality with an advancement of Unity in different states of existence in different degrees. In the words of Varma, we may evaluate this humanistic programme in the context of the examination of the spontaneous development of *Humanism* in India. Varma observes, "Humanism is opposed to credel denominationalism and theological orthodoxy or ecclesiastical fanaticism. The external ritualism of religions leaves it cold. It craves for personal piety and simple modes of difference-offering. To it, no caste or race or nation has the monopoly of reason or wisdom. In their protest against the ritualist mathematics of the sacrificers, the sages of the Upanishads, Mahavira, Makkhali Gosala and Buddha marked a humanist protest. Against the Puranic cosmogonies and conflicts of the gods, the leaders of the Nirguna Bhakti School like Kabir and Nanak heralded a humanist protest in the name of the weaker and despised sections of the contemporary society. In the face of the sanction of social cruelties and illogical statements by the narrow-minded legists like Parasara, Kamalakara and Raghunandana, the exponents of renascent Indian spirit like Ram Mohan, Dayananda, Ramakrishna, Vivekananda, Shraddhananda, Rama Tirth, Narayana Swami and others marked a quest for deep tolerance, comprehensive universality and inclusive brotherhood."[34] In this humanistic development, we observe the supreme existence of man with "...deep tolerance and comprehensive universality" with an extension of the human relation as an 'inclusive brotherhood.' These, in the observation of Vivekananda, are the real bases of man that make him infinite and spiritual. The infinite potency of man as his spiritual nature, expressed through different creative states of existence in multidimensional forms and manners, can manifest his universality. This on one hand, makes him tolerant in several contradictions of life and society and on the other hand helps him to overcome these contradictions through the development of human values with the proper expansion of the humanistic relation of unity. In the observation of Radhakrishnan, this philosophy of Man, The Spiritual of Vivekananda, may be evaluated thus, "It is human nature that has brought about all the great changes that have taken place in this world. And if there is any call which Vivekananda made to us, it is to rely on our own spiritual resources. Say that man has inexhaustible spiritual resources. His spirit is supreme, man is unique. There is nothing inevitable in this world, and we can ward off the worst dangers and worst disabilities by which we are faced. Only we should not loose hope. He gave us fortitude in suffering, he gave us hope in distress, he gave us courage in despair. He told us: "Do not be led away by the appearances. Deep down there is a providential will, there is a purpose in this universe: You must try to cooperate with that purpose and try to achieve it."[35] In the background of these observations it may be pointed out that the fundamental object of Vivekananda's philosophy of Man, The Spiritual is to overcome all contradictions or evils of life as appearances and to realize the reality as the infinite or spiritual nature of man that creates the fearlessness and tolerance in human existence, making him more dynamic and creative in changing those evils and contradictions in a harmonious form of developing unity and universality. This is the only basis of the *Spiritual Humanism*, as founded and developed by Swami Vivekananda. In the words of Varma, this type of philosophy of *Humanism* is finally examined in the following way. Varma observes, "It is the culmination of reverence for the dignity of man. It is the supreme affirmation of the creative dynamic spontaneity of man attained by encountering reality with heroic courage and realistic spirit. Plato's Republic, Hobbes's Leviathan and Hegel's Philosophy of Right do not contain any concept that can be equated with the Vedic concept of *abhayam. Abhayam* enshrines a higher ideal for realisation *than* the concept of liberty cherished by John Stuart Mill, Green and Laski. Idealist Humanism upholds *abhayam* as its fundamental value and supports on metaphysical foundations."[36]

The cultivation of this spirit of *Abhayam* or fearlessness as revealed in *Vedic* and Indian culture, is to develop the infinite and creative spirit of man as Man, The Spiritual that is evaluated by Vivekananda in his programme of the religion of man, as the realisation of universality, not as an imposition of some ideas or ideals on man but as the expression of universality in individual or collective existence. With this idea of Man, The Spiritual with its creative inter-cultural prospect in the development of *Spiritual Humanism*, Varma rightly thinks, "...the protagonist of idealist humanism is sanguine that the teachings of the great political philosophers of the East and the West on the concept of man as moral and spiritual subject must have their impact on providing the enlarged frame of mind and the strength of will needed to ride over the crisis and challenges."[37]

Notes and References

1. *Complete Works of Swami Vivekananda,* Sixth Edition, Vol. III, p. 221.
2. Swami Ranganathananda, *Eternal Values for a Changing Society,* 1958, pp. 111-115.

3. *Complete Works of Swami Vivekananda* , Fifth Edition, Vol.VII, p. 148.
4. *Complete Works of Swami Vivekananda,* Birth Centenary Edition, 1963, Vol. IV, p. 468.
5. Swami Vivekananda Studies in Soviet Union, 1987, p. 210.
6. Ryazanskaya, S. (Ed), The *German Ideology-Karl Marx and Frederick Engels,* 1964, pp. 44-45.
7. Marx, *Economic and Philosophical Manuscripts* of 1844, 1974, pp. 64-70.
8. *Complete Works of Swami Vivekananda,* Almora, 1965, Vol. V, p. 14.
9. *Complete Works of Swami Vivekananda,* Almora, 1965, Vol. IV, pp. 468-69.
10. *Ibid.*
11. *Complete Works of Swami Vivekananda,* Alrnora, 1965, Vol. I, p. 124.
12. Swami Vivekananda, *Patravalee,* Vol. II, 1367 B.S., p. 164.
13. *Ibid.,* p. 164.
14. *Banee O Racana,* 1st Edition. Vol. III, pp. 344-50.
15. *Ibid.*
16. B. Russell, *History of Western Philosophy,1967.* p. 691.
17. Romain Rolland, *The Life of Vivekananda and the Universal Gospel,* 1979, p. 288.
18. *Complete Worlds of Swami Vivekananda,* Birth Cent. Edn., Vol. V, p. 138.
19. Romain Rolland, *The Life of Vivekananda and the Universe Gospel,* 1979, pp. 287-288.
20. Swami Ranganathananda, *Swami Vivekananda His Humanism,* 1982, p. 37.
21. *Ibid.,* p. 35.
22. *Sri Aurobindo Birth Centenary,* Library, Pondicherry, 1973, Vol.: XXVII, p. 435.
23. Swami Vivekananda Studies in Soviet Union, 1987, pp. 128-129
24. *Complete Works of Swami Vivekananda,* 1959, Vol. VIII, p. 76.
25. Swami Vivekananda Studies in Soviet Union, 1987, pp. 208-9.
26. S. Radhiikrishan, *Indian Phi1osophy,* Vol. I, 1971, pp. 360-361.
27. Satis Chandra Chatterjee, *Classical Indian Philosophies: Their synthesis in the philosophy* of *Sri Ramakrishna,* 1963, p. 17.
28. Anil Kumar Sarkar, *Changing Phases of Buddhist Thought* (A Study in the Background of East-West Philosophy), 3rd Edn. 1983, p. 288.
29. Satis Chandra Chatterjee, *Classical Indian Philosophies,* 1963, p. 16.
30. Gobinda Chandra Dev, Swami Vivekananda's Ethics of Renunciation, *Vivekananda Centenary Memorial Volume,* 1987, p. 337.

31. Asit Kumar Bandyopadhyay, *Unisnbish,* 1374. B. S., p. 174.
32. *Encyclopedia Britannica,* 1969, Vol.VIII, p. 965.
33. *Complete Works of Swami Vivekananda,* 1958. Vol. Il, pp. 301-02.
34. V. P. Varma, *Philosophical Humanism and Contemporary India,* 1979, pp. 50-51.
35. *Ibid,* pp. 7-8.
36. *Swami Vivekananda Centenary Memorial Volume,* 1983, pp. X-XI.
37. V. P. Varma, *Philosophical Humanism and Contemporary India*, 1979, p. 10.

Chapter - 4

Concluding Observations on Man, The Spiritual: An Intercultural Expansion of Swami Vivekananda's Synthetic Vision of Humanity

Problems and Prospect of Swami Vivekananda's Intercultural Ideal, a Reality

After a careful analysis of the humanistic thought of Vivekananda, as reflected through his life and activities it is found that, he, like all other contemporary Indian thinkers, tries to establish a neo-outlook of the philosophy of man as the religion of humanity which is the fundamental basis of Indian philosophy and culture. But in the analysis of this new outlook of the philosophy of religion, he tries to reform the old and traditional view of religion and also tries to change the so-called usages of religion as supernatural and superhuman values which are to be imposed upon man from without.

Religion on the other hand, as Vivekananda observes, as the religion of man, is a natural process of life which is purely human, as it is intimately related to the life of human beings. There is a gradual development in the process of human life, which, according to Swamiji, is a process of becoming through which a man realises his own existence in and through the contradictions of this material world. This realisation of his own existence as Man among contradictions, is the essence of religion and philosophy which is to grow from within that is to know and to realise the intrinsic spiritual nature of man. This process of life, according to Swamiji, is not unnatural or supernatural, but on the other hand it is the natural expression of human life in different states of existence, manifesting potential universality. So, religion in this humanistic sense, may be taken as the history of human existence as it is the development of human life in different ages.

In this way, by accepting religion as the expression and the development of human nature and existence, Vivekananda expands the essential spirit of the religion of humanity, making religion intimate to human life when he observes that human life stands on religion and religion on the other hand is the natural expression of the life of man. So this humanistic approach of Vivekananda finally makes religion as the religion of man.

For the analysis of the proper nature of the religion of man, Vivekananda tries to explain the nature and character of human life which, in his observation, is the only basis of religion and philosophy. Man, according to Swamiji, is both material and spiritual in nature. The material existence of man shows that as man exists in this material world, he must have material demands of life which he wants to fulfill. But mere fulfillment of these material demands, Swami ji observes, expresses the ego of man that makes him limited and finite. This finite procedure of life through mere satisfaction of material desires, create contradictions or disunites in human life and society. As man has an existence in this material world, material contradictions in human life are relatively real and thus cannot be ignored or avoided. But reality or truth does not lie in these apparent contradictions only, on the other hand, it lies in the potential power of transcending the finiteness or limitation through which man can develop his potential infiniteness and thus can overcome the contradictions or disunities in life and existence. This, according to Vivekananda, is the expression of the inner spirit of man, and that expresses the spiritual existence of man who is potentially Infinite or Universal. The essential nature of man is to develop this infiniteness or universality in this life and world which is the fundamental end of the religion of man and for this Swamiji expresses, 'Religion is neither word, nor doctrine. It is to be and become…'

Thus, in developing the infinite or universal nature of man, Vivekananda points out that the religion as the expression of this universality of man also becomes universal, which on the one hand, tries to reconcile different contradictions in human life and society through the expression of universality as unity in human life and society, and it, on the other hand, also tries to unite or synthesise different values and ideals as introduced by the different religions and philosophies of the world for the development of harmony as universality in religion as religion of humanity.

So, the harmonious development of the religion of humanity, expressing universality, stands on a synthetic idea. If its nature or character is carefully examined, we may find its proper expression in different states of human existence. Through the development of this idea as synthesis and through its expression in life and activities, Swamiji tries to explain the nature of human life in a synthetic manner, when he follows a synthetic system of thought, introduced by different Indian thinkers in their coherent and consistent development. This process of analysis urges Swamiji to explain every sphere of life critically in the background of this broad synthetic outlook. In this way he tries to synthesise all the common elements or values of life for the harmonious development of human life and existence. This process of harmonisation, according to Swamiji, a critical analysis of life and society, for a proper reconciliation of contradictions or evils in a highest human value of harmony.

Thus, through this synthetic programme, Swamiji explains and evaluates the nature and existence of man more systematically. Man exists in this material world and faces material contradictions. But the humanistic development of life, as Vivekananda observes, lies in the reconciliation of contradictions through the synthetic expression of potential perfection which is spiritual in nature. Thus man, in the observation of Vivekananda, is both material and spiritual in nature. But these two opposite elements in man do not create any contradiction as both of them are harmonised in the highest state of human life when a man becomes Man the universal or Infinite. In this stage of universality a man can overcome all his material contradictions or disharmonies of life through the proper development of perfection as unity in him which, according to Vivekananda, is the expression of the divinity of Man as Man, The Spiritual.

God in this spiritualistic process, is taken as the central element which is explained by Vivekananda as the creative synthesis of the theistic and the absolutistic values. Like Dr J. Royce, a Western thinker, Vivekananda also evaluates the idea of God as a substratum of values which is harmoniously manifested in human life in different degrees. This type of spiritual programme of developing values in manifestation of God as human values in human life, gradually introduces the harmonisation of values as the synthesis of divinity and humanity in man and society.

So, God, in this sense, is empirically real as he is manifested in man as human values in different degrees in different stages of human life, where we find the theistic approach of God through the introduction of duality between God and man, because man as a finite being tries to realise this infinite value in different states of life. But this realisation proceeds towards the introduction of the ideal of non-duality through the inauguration of idea of God as one of Absolute Unity or Identity. Vivekananda explains, "Personal God is as much an entity for Himself as we are for ourselves, and no more. God can also be seen as a form, just as we are seen. As men we must need God, as gods we need none. This is why Sri Ramakrishna constantly saw the Divine Mother ever present with him, more real than anything around him; but in Samadhi all went but the self. Personal God comes nearer and nearer until He melts away and there is no personal God and no more "I", all is merged in the self."[1] So, realisation of God, as Swamiji observes, is a synthetic process of life which proceeds through the gradual manifestations of divine values in different stages of existence towards the highest manifestation of absolute unity. Thus, it may be noted in this connection that Vivekananda, like all other contemporary Indian thinkers, evaluates the idea of God as the central element of synthesis. In his observation, this idea, in one hand, synthesises Theistic, Absolutistic and all other approaches to God and in other, this synthetic process leads to the introduction of unity or harmony in human existence. In this connection it may be said that there is an influence of synthetic idea in Rabindranath Tagore, who like Swamiji, also explains the nature and existence of God and man in a synthetic form, introducing his philosophy of the Religion of Man as the divinity of man and the humanity of god. In this context it may also be pointed out that if we examine the intrinsic element of contemporary Indian thought, we shall find it as a synthetic process, in analysing God and man. For this Srivastava rightly observes, "Along with his philosophy we find that the characteristic of the great contemporary Indian philosophers viz. Dr Radhakrishnan, Mahatma Gandhi, Vivekananda and Sri Aurobindo lies in accepting both the theistic and the absolutistic aspects of God as real, and in evolving synthetic systems of philosophy."[2]

Thus, Vivekananda, like all other contemporary Indian thinkers, puts much importance on the synthetic development of life where God is taken as central force of unity. The realisation of God in man is the realisation of perfection in different degrees and that proceeds towards the final realisation of Unity which is to be recognised as the realisation of one or self as Non-dual or Absolute. This is the highest state of life which may be said as the final state of human freedom when there will be the inauguration of the feeling of unity or harmony in human existence.

For the introduction of this highest state of human freedom, Vivekananda also puts an importance on the human procedure of life in a synthetic manner which, according to him, is possible through the disinterested and unconditional process of life which, in his observation, is love and service to mankind. Other procedures of human life may not help a man to develop his total perfection being conditional processes, as these may develop attachment or egoism in man, responsible for creating contradictions in social life. For this, Swamiji introduces the ideal of disinterested love for man, which produces detachment or ideal of renunciation in man that helps him to love all beings as the expressions of god that inspires man to love and work for others unconditionally. Swamiji observes, "to love living beings, is to serve God." Thus, the ideal method of love introduces an unconditional process of developing the divinity in man as it helps a man to develop his potential nature of love as perfection, which, in the final state of development, introduces a synthesis of man and God or Absolute in the disinterested feeling of self-less love for the universal mankind, leading to the realisation of the absolute value of love as perfect Bliss *or Anandam.* Through this selfless process, an individual man realises his potential greatness or universality and finally becomes the great or Universal Man. Through the inauguration of universality in human life, the human society also becomes free from narrow contradictions and thus through the development of unity in men, a social unity may also be developed that makes the spirituality of life as the unity of materiality and divinity on earth possible.

In this connection, it may be pointed out that this selfless process of the philosophy of man which is evaluated by Vivekananda as the religion of humanity, may also be called as the religion of love as it helps a man to express his spirit of love towards the development of the highest state of perfection as unity in contradictions in individual life. This also introduces unity in social life of men through unconditional service for others, making one more intimate with all.

So this selfless and unconditional programme of love and service cultivates a spirit of detachment in man, manifesting his potential perfection. This makes a man to be more and more intimate with others that urges him to work for all in an unconditional manner. So the unconditional spirit in love develops a selfless process of service. Thus, the joint process of love and service in an unconditional form relates one with all, developing eternal relation among men in society. In this way he becomes the great lover of mankind and gradually becomes the world worker for the establishment of unity or harmony in society. It manifests the spirit of universality in man, advancing harmony in men and society.

This process of expressing universality and unity, in the observation of Vivekananda, is a synthetic process of expanding divinity in man as non-duality of man and God or Absolute. Vivekananda evaluates it as a socio-spiritual unity of transcendental value of God or Absolute through the experiential programme of man in love and service.

Thus, the transcendent-experiential process of developing unity, solves different social and moral problems of life due to limitations and material contradictions. The development of mere materiality through a mere satisfaction of particular material demand of life, may create a contrast between individual's interest and social interest which is a proper cause of moral and social problems in human life. But the ideals of selfless love and service for others developing potential perfection in man, inspire him to sacrifice his poor interest for the greater cause of social justice and equality. The establishment of these ideals requires a synthetic development of man that, according to

Swamiji, can be possible through the advancement of human life on a social value with its synthetic expression in love and service. This synthetic process develops man's greater or social self over and above the poor ego or narrow material interest of life overcoming all the contradictions caused by those limited interests. The significance of overcoming these narrow limitations and contradictions lies in a proper introduction of unity or harmony in individual and collective or social life of man that, as Vivekananda observes, is the development of human freedom.

So, the fundamental object of Vivekananda's philosophy of Man, The Spiritual is the advancement of human freedom through the expansion of the inner spirit of man in love and service. These ideals relate the traditional idea of religion with the humanistic processes. The synthesis of the religion and life with an expression in humanistic activities thus can be recognised as expansion of the religion of humanity. In this way the final end of Vivekananda's idea of the religion of man as the religion of humanity is to introduce humanistic philosophy for peace in a harmonious development of life and existence. Dr Radhakrishnan rightly observes, "Peace is the harmonising of men in their differences..."[3]

The humanistic analysis of the philosophy of peace in this sense, is explained as the harmonisation of human values in differences. This humanistic process of developing harmony is evaluated by Rabindranath Tagore, as the "Meditation on humanity", which, in the observation of Sri Ramakrishna, as the inauguration of divine unity as humanity.

The ideas of god and man, according to these Indian thinkers, are nothing but the synthetic expressions of the ideas of divinity and humanity in human existence. The manifestations of humanity in man and society in different degrees is a gradual expression of divinity as transcendent value of unity or harmony. Sri Ramakrishna explains this process that mere work for the fulfillment of poor self-interest is the expression of *Jeevabhava* which creates contradiction in life and society. But *Devabhava,* as he points out, is the fundamental idea of man which, in the analysis of Vivekananda, is closely associated with the humanistic idea that inspires man to work for greater self or for the welfare of the mankind, realising unity in contradictions of life and existence.

In the evaluation of divinity and humanity as synthetic idea, Vivekananda points out that it is also closely related to the synthetic expression in humanistic knowledge and activities, leading to the inauguration of synthetic existence when one observes others in his own existence and also realises him in the existence of others. This is the development of the spirit of unity and non-duality of man and God or Absolute which is examined in the system of *Advaita Vedanta* as '*Sarvam Khalvidam Brahma*'. Vivekananda observes the expression of this synthetic ideal of unity and universality in all men in all societies. Any system of philosophy or religion which expresses this synthetic ideal for selfless activity, is accepted by him. This synthetic spirit of Swamiji thus cultivates a spirit of democratic value or ideal which was examined by his master Sri Ramakrishna as '*Yata mat tata path*'. Any particular system of thought which explains the truth from its particular standpoint, becomes a limited and particular *mat* or opinion and *path* or way. But in the background of universal truth or humanistic ideal for total welfare of men and society, there will be a creative synthesis among different opinions and ways, facts and philosophies or religions, life and activities. Through this creative synthesis in a creative humanistic programme, Vivekananda observes the active development of human freedom in peace.

In this creative, synthetic and humanistic process, Vivekananda also directed his programme for developing ideal state as the synthetic development of human essence, making a proper equilibrium of different qualities and actions of people of different communities. This expresses the creative essence of the *Spiritual Socialism* as advanced by Vivekananda, which may be observed as a democratic process of developing equality and unity as transcendent ideal or value through different experiential processes. Swami Ranganathananda evaluates this programme in following manner: "But when you come to the modern understanding of democracy- viewed through the Indian cultural heritage- you see a new value coming in. That value, is the integral value of every human being. Nobody has a fractional value, everybody has an integral value. This is the beautiful part of democracy."[4]

The inner significance of this programme is not to develop a particular class through the elimination of other classes or communities. For this, in the analysis of the upliftment of the life of proletariat or *Shudras,* Vivekananda does not suggest the introduction of a particular system. He, on the other hand, prescribes, "The rising of the shudra class, with their shudra-hood." The social significance of this programme is the synthetic existence and development of shudras with their qualities and actions as "Shudra-hood" in a harmony with other qualities and actions of other communities in a society. For proper evaluation of this process, Sri Mazumdar points out, "It does not require much logic to demonstrate that Vedanta paves the way towards socialism. When Vivekananda declared 'I am a socialist' all that he meant was the *Vedantic Socialism* which preaches oneness of existence and breaks down all artificial barriers between man and man, between race and race."[5] It may be noted in this connection that this type of the *Vedantic* form of socialism is nothing but the humanistic process of developing unity in human existence.

The importance of this humanistic process lies in the harmonious development of human personality in a transcendent-experiential process when man can realise the truth as human effort to realise a perfect condition which is man's potentiality to be infinite by overcoming all restrictions and limitations. So the creative essence of man is the realisation of infiniteness or universality as the transcendental value of unity with its experiential process in harmony of values in men and communities through a proper reconciliation of contradictions due to limitations or finiteness in human existence.

Thus, it may pointed out that it is a process of manifesting human freedom in the cultivation of universality as the expression of natural potency of man. So its significance lies in the self-transcendence of finiteness as the material contradictions or evils with the self-manifestation of potential universality in the harmonious development of human existence as good. This idea of good as the integrated development of man with the reconciliation of contradictions or evils in human existence, prepares a proper ground for national integration as the harmonisation of values of different men and communities, expanding the national value of good as intercultural community or one nation.

In the same way this intercultural programme for expanding the philosophy of integration in the international state of existence as the intercommunication of different nations and states, also prepares a firm ground for developing creative integration as reconciliation of differences, founding world unity as *World Community*.

So today when our world is facing the crisis, arising out of the problems of war and peace, Vivekananda's humanistic philosophy of integration will make the programme of developing *World Community,* as suggested by modern sociologists and political philosophers, more effective and fruitful. In their sociological analysis, thc modern sociologists like R.M. MacIver and Charles H. Page also evaluate this programme in a rational and synthetic manner. They explain this possibility thus: "Certainly Wendell Willkie's *One World* has been in the making for centuries. We have been approaching a stage where no completely self-contained community can be found on any scale unless we extend the limits of community to include the whole earth."[6] The extension of the limits of communities means the expansion of the prospective process of intercommunication. Through the intercommunication of different socio-cultural values and ideas of different nations and communities, there will be a humanistic development of intercultural unity.

This idea of unity, as Vivekananda observes, is not an artificial or external bond to be imposed upon men and communities from outside. It, on the other hand, is an internal and essential development as related to the harmonious expression of creative universality in man which, in the observation of Vivekananda, is spiritual from a transcendent-experiential perspective. This may be said as the humanistic programme of experiencing transcendent value of unity or universality with harmonious development of men and nations as the harmonisation of values and ideas which, in the observation of Vivekananda, is purely human in nature.

So the meaning and nature of Vivekananda's philosophy of the religion of man as harmonious development of man with the harmonisation of human values, finally stand on *Humanism*, containing the unity of men and world. Varma evaluates this process, "...humanism on the global scale demands that the future world order should not annihilate diversity and multiformity but should seek to stress the foundational principle of human unity on moral, political, sociological and economic considerations."[7]

For this "human unity" there should be a cultivation of human values which in the observation of Tarkunde, is the expansion of "The social ideal of humanism" as "to help in creating a society of free and moral men and women."[8] This is a democratic process of expanding *Humanism* which, in observation of M. N. Roy, is radical in nature. This has been evaluated by Tarkunde with its prospective development. He writes "Radical Humanism defends the limited democracy of today in order that it may he transformed into a comprehensive political, economic and social democracy of the future."[9]

This comprehensive development of democratic values, according to Vivekananda, is spiritual in expanding the philosophy of *Spiritual Humanism*. It includes the development of the individual, the social and the spiritual existence of man through the cultivation of transcendent value of unity in diverse processes of experience in different degrees. But this finally leads to the development of creative unity in multidimensional forms as diversities with the expression of universality in peace which, in the observation of Vivekananda, is the expansion of divine world order. Radhakrishnan evaluates this divine or spiritual process thus: "Let us live in the world of time, have the perspective of the eternal, discipline ourselves so that every act we do, we do it as a dedication to the eternal. And all our activities are to be utilised for the purpose of producing better life, a creative life, in which every man will have more amplitude of existence, more richness of being, more fervour of friendship."[10]

In the background of this evaluation of the '...the purpose of producing better life and creative life', Man, in the observation of Vivekananda, is a '*being*' which is purely creative. So, it may finally be said that the philosophy of *Spiritual Humanism* of Swamiji, expounding the creative nature of '*being*' is very much unique and distinct from Western idea of *Humanism*. Vivekananda's idea of spirituality is the '*becoming*' of the creative state of '*being*'. In this process of creativity, Man becomes Creator as Man, The Spiritual or

God. So, Swamiji's philosophy of Man, is a direct, active and creative in the form of transforming the human existence in an expansion of the idea of *Spiritual Humanism*. But, *Humanism*, in Western context, is a passive state of human existence in acquiring some human qualities. Man, in the observation of Vivekananda, on the other hand is purely active and creative state of existence in developing his spiritual or infinite potentiality of '*becoming*' universal. Thus, *Spiritual Humanism* in this context, is to be evaluated as the Theory of Creative Man or '*Sristisheel Manavbad*'. The expounding of creative '*being*' means to develop Harmony as the creative synthesis of human values in different states of human existence which, in the opinion of Radhakrishnan, a contemporary Indian thinker, is the expansion of '*Peace*' as Harmony in differences. In this creative process of Harmony, there is an opening of the sprite of universal humanity in reconciling all differences or contradictions in life and existence. Here lies the significance of Vivekananda's philosophy of creative Man, The Spiritual, Infinite or Universal in cultivating harmony in an intercultural form with a prospect of developing universal humanity.

Notes and References

1. *The Complete Works of Swami Vivekananda,* Almora, 1951, Vol. II, p. 55.
2. R. S. Srivastava, *Contemporary Indian Philosophy,* 1965, p. 88.
3. S. Radhakrishnan, Art A Quest for Peace, *"The Creative Life"* (Orient Paperbacks) 1975, p. 63.
4. Swami Ranganathananda, Swami Vivekananda's Socialism, *Bulletin* of *the Ramakrishna Mission Institute of Culture,* Commemorative Number, February, 1992, p. 63.
5. A. K. Mazumdar, *Swami Vivekananda as a Vedantist,* March, 1991, p. 26.
6. Maclver R. M. and Page Charles H., *Society,* 1962, p. 11.
7. V. P. Varma, *Philosophical Humanism and Comparative India,* 1979, p. 113.
8. Tarkunde, V. M., *Radical Humanism, The Philosophy of Freedom and Democracy,* 1983, p. 4.
9. *Ibid.,* p. 5.
10. S. Radhakrishnan, *The Creative Life* (Orient Paperback), 1975, p. 11.

A Select Bibliography
Works of Vivekananda

In Bengali

Yanma Satavarser Smarane, Swami Vivekanander Bani O *Rachana, Vols. I-X,* Udbodhan Karyalayay, Calcutta, 1369 B. S.

In English

Complete Works of Swami Vivekananda, Birth Centenary Edition, Vols. I-VIII, Advaita Ashrama, Calcutta, 1963.

Works on Vivekananda

In Bengali

Basu, S. P., *Vivekananda O Samakalin Bharatvarsa,* Vols. I-VII, Mandal Book House, Calcutta, 1975-1987.

Dutta, B.N., *Swami Vivekananda,* Nababharat Publishers, Calcutta, 1393 B.S.

Ghosh, P. R., *Vivekananda O Banglasahitya,* Karuna Prakashani, Calcutta, 19630.

Majumdar, M., *Vir Sanyasi Vivekananda,* General Books, Calcutta, 1963.

Majumdar, *S., Vivekananda Charit,* Ananda Publishers, Calcutta, 1919.

Mitra Kautilya, *Vivekanander Viplab Chinta,* Sujan Publications, Calcutta, 1982.

Marx O-Vivekananda, Sujan Publications, Calcutta, 1984.

Niramayananda, S., *Chotader Vivekananda,* Swami Vivekananda Satavarsiki, Calcutta, 1963.

Roy, T. R., *Vivekanander Siksa Chinta,* General Books, Calcutta, 1963.

Roy Chaudhuri, G. S., *Swami Vivekananda O Banglar Unabingsa Satabdi,* Nababharat Publishers, Calcutta, 1927.

Someswarananda, S, *Itihas Chintaya Vivekananda,* Sraddha Prakashan, Calcutta,1983.

In English

Abhedananda, S, *Swami Vivekananda and His Works,* Ramakrishna Vivekananda Math, Calcutta, 1950.

Bure, M. L., *Swami Vivekananda in America,* New Discoveries, Advaita Ashrama, Calcutta, 1958.

Das, T, *Social Philosophy of Swami Vivekananda,*Co-operative Book Depot, Calcutta, 1949.

Dasgupta, S., *Vivekananda: The Prophet of Human Emancipation,* Golf Green, Calcutta, 1991.

Dutta, B. N., *Swami Vivekananda, Patriot and Prophet,* Nababharat Press, Calcutta, 1954.

Eastern and Western Disciples, *Life of Swami Vivekananda* (in one Volume), Advaita Ashrama, Calcutta, 1912.

Majumdar, A. K., *Understanding Vivekananda,* Sanskrit Pustak Bhandar, Calcutta, 1972.

Swami Vivekananda as a Vedantist, Vivekananda Kendra Publication, Kanyakumari, 1991.

Nehru, J., *Sri Ramakrishna and Swami Vivekananda,* Advaita Ashrama, Mayavati, 1949.

Nikhilananda, S., *Vivekananda-A Biography,* Ramakrishna-Vivekananda Centre, New York, 1953.

Nivedita, S., *The Master-as I saw him,* Udbodhan, Calcutta, 1948.

Nivedita, S., *Notes of Some Wanderings with Swami Vivekananda,* Udbodhan, Calcutta, 1913.

Parameswaran, P., *Marx and Vivekananda,* Sterling Publishers (P) Ltd., New Delhi, 1987.

Ranganathananda, S., *Swami Vivekananda-His Humanism,* Moscow University Lecture, Advaita Ashrama, Calcutta, 1982.

Reddy, A. V. R., *The Political Philosophy of Swami Vivekananda,* Sterling Publishers, New Delhi, 1984.

Rolland, R., *The Life of Vivekananda and the Universal Gospel,* Vol. II, Advaita Ashrama, Calcutta, 1979.

Yale, J., *What Religion Is In The Words of Vivekananda,* Phoenix, London, 1963.

Other Works

In Bengali

Bagal, Y. C., *Benglar Navya Samskriti,* Visvabharati Granthalaya, Calcutta, 1958.

Bhattacharya, U. C., *Charsa Bacharer Paschatya Darshan,* Jijnasa, Calcutta, 1980.

Dasgupta, S. B., *Bharatiya Sadhanar Aikya,* Visvabharati Granthan Bibhag, Calcutta, 1899.

Roy, S., *Bharater Vaiplabik Sangramer Itihas,* Vol. I, DNBA Brothers, Calcutta, 1970.

Roy, P. R., *Bijnan Darshan O Dharma,* Jijnasa, Calcutta, 1983.

Sri Ma (Mahendra Gupta) Kathita, *Sri Ramakrishna Kathamrita,* Parts I-V, Kathamrita Bhavan, Calcutta, 1379 B. S.

Tarkabhusan, M. P., *Srimadhbhagavadgeeta,* Dev Sahitya Kutir Private Limited, Calcutta, 1973.

In English

Aurobindo, *Foundations of Indian Culture,* Sri Aurobindo Ashram, Pondicherry, 1972.

Abhedananda, S., *Self Knowledge,* Vedanta Society, New York, 1905.

Afanssyev, V., *Marxist Philosophy, A Popular Outline,* Progress Publishers, Moscow,1980.

Ahmad, H. M. G., *The Philosophy of the Teachings of Islam,* Qadian, Punjab, India, 1965.

Bahm, A. J., *Comparative Philosophy,* World Books, Albuquerque, USA, 1977.

Barlingay, S. S., *Poverty, Power, Progress,* Panchsheel Publishers, New Delhi,1983.

Banerjee, N. V., The *Concept of Philosophy,* University of Calcutta, Calcutta, 1968.

Basu, M., *Ramakrishna Sadhan Parikrama,* Kalighat, Calcutta, 1981.

Blackham, H. J., *Six Existentialist Thinkers,* Routledge & Kegan Paul Ltd., London, 1972.

Bosanquet, B., *The Value and Destiny of the Individual,* Macmillan & Co. Ltd., London, 1913.

Caird, J., *An Introduction to the Philosophy of Religion,* Chuckervorty, Chatterjee & Co. Ltd., Calcutta, 1956.

Chatterjee, S. C., *Classical Indian Philosophies, Their Synthesis in the Philosophy of Sri Ramakrishna,* University of Calcutta, Calcutta, 1963.

Chatterjee, P. B., *Studies in Comparative Religion,* Das Gupta & Co. Private Ltd., Calcutta, 1971.

Chattopadhyay, D. P., *What is Living and What is Dead in Indian Philosophy,* People's Publishing House, New Delhi, 1977.

Chattopadhyay, S. N., *The Universal Man, Tagore's Vision of the Religion* of *Humanity,* Naya Prokash, Calcutta, 1987.

Chakravorti, A., *The Idealist Theory of Value,* University of Calcutta, Calcutta, 1966.

Das, A. C., *A Modem Incarnation of God,* General Printers & Publishers Private Limited, Calcutta, 1958.

Das, B., *Essential Unity of All Religions,* Bharatiya Vidya Bhavan, Bombay, 1960 .

Dasgupta, S. N., *History of Indian Philosophy,* Vols. I - V, Cambridge University Press, 1922-1956.

Dhar, N., *Vedanta and Bengal Renaissance*, Minarva Associates (Publications) Pvt. Ltd., Calcutta, 1977.

Edwards, D.M., *The Philosophy of Religion*, Progressive Publishers, Calcutta, 1960.

Ewing, A.C., *The Fundamental Questions of Philosophy*, Allied Publishers Private Limited, New Delhi, 1982.

Farquhar, J.N., *Modern Religious Movements in India*, Macmillan & Co. Ltd. London, 1929.

Faucett, L., *Six Great Teachers of Morality*, Shirozaki Shorin, Tokyo, 1958.

Gisbert, P., *Fundamentals of Sociology,* Orient Longmans, Calcutta, 1959.

Gupta, H.C., *Swami Vivekananda Studies in Soviet Union*, The Ramakrishna Mission Institute of Culture, Calcutta, 1987.

Hiriyanna, M., *Essentials of Indian Philosophy*, Vikas Publishing House Pvt. Ltd., New Delhi, 1974.

Huxley, J.S., *Religion without Revealation*, Ernest Benn Ltd., London, 1927.

Hutchison, J.A. and Martin, J.A., *Ways of faith*, Ronald Press, New York, 1953.

Ilitskaya, L., *ABC of Dialectical and Historical Materialism*, Progress Publishers, Mascow, 1978.

Isherwood, C., *Ramakrishna and His Disciples*, Advaita Ashrama, Calcutta, 1980.

Jagadananda, S., *Sri Ramakrishna–The Great Master by Swami Sharadananda*, Sri Ramakrishna Math, Mylapur, Madras, 1952.

James, W., *Pragmatism*, Longmans, Green and Co. New York, 1916.

Jalil Mia, A., *A Contemporary Philosophy of Religion*, Islamic Foundation, Bangladesh, 1982.

Lotze, H., *Outlines of the Philosophy of Religion*, Chuckerverty Chatterjee & Co. Ltd., Calcutta, 1954.

Leonhard, W., *Three Faces of Marxism*, Holt, Rinehart and Winston, New York, 1974.

MacIver, R., M, and Page, C.H., *Society*, Macmillan & Co. Ltd., London, 1962.

Maclcolm Smity, E.F., *Prophets of New India by Romain Rolland*, Cassell, London, 1930.

Mackenzie, J.S., *Outlines of Social Philosophy*, George Allen and Unwin, London, 1961.

Majumdar, R.C., *History of the Freedom Movement in India*, Firma K.L. Mukhopadhyay, Calcutta, 1962.

Maitra, S.K., *Religious Essayes*, University of Calcutta, 1964.

The Main Problem of Philosophy, An Advaita Approach, Part Two, Progressive Publishers, Calcutta, 1962.

Marx, K., *Economic and Philosophic Manuscript of 1844,* Progress Publishers, Moscow, 1977.

Marx, K., and Engels, Fu, *Manifesto of the Communist Party,* Progress Publishers, Moscow, 1975.

Muller, M., *Ramkrishna-His Life and Sayings,* Advaita Ashrama, Almora, 1951.

Meszaros, I., *Marx's Theory of Alienation,* Merlin Press, London, 1982.

Nagaraja Rao, P., *Contemporary Indian Philosophy;* Bharatiya Vidya Bhavan, Bombay, 1970.

Nikhilananda, S., *The Gospel of Sri Ramakrishna,* Sri Ramakrishna Math, Mylapur, Madras, 1974.

Otto, R., *The Idea of the Holy,* Penguin Books Pvt. Ltd. London, 1959.

Oizerman, T. I., Bogomolv, A. S., *Principles of the Theory of the Historical Process in Philosophy,* Progress Publishers, Moscow, 1986.

Panikker, S. K. M., *The Determining Periods of Indian History,* Bharatiya Vidya Bhavan, Bombay, 1962.

Pringle-Pattison, A.S., *The Idea of God,* Academic Publishers, Calcutta, 1967.

Paton, H. J., *The Categorical Imperative, A study in Kant's Moral Philosophy,* Hutchinson of London, 1970.

Ranganathananda, S., *Eternal Values for a Changing Society,* Bharatiya Vidya Bhavan, Bombay, 1971.

Radhakrishnan, S., *Science and Religion,* Advaita Ashrama, Calcutta, 1982.

Radhakrishnan, S., *Indian Philosophy,* Vols, I&II, George Allen & Unwin Ltd., London, 1992, 1931.

Radhakrishnan, S., *Religion and Society,* George Allen & Unwin Ltd., London, 1959.

Rolland, R., *The Life of Ramakrishna,* Vol. I, Advaita Ashrama, Calcutta 1979.

Royce, J., *The World and the Individual,* Dover Publications, Inc, New York, 1959.

Russell, B., *History of Western Philosophy,* Allen & Unwin, London, 1967.

Sahakian, W. S., Sahakian, M. L., *Ideas of the Great Philosophies,* Barnes & Noble, Inc. New York, 1967.

Sardesai, S. G. and Bose, D., *Marxism and Bhagvat Geeta,* People's Publishing House, New Delhi, 1982.

Sarkar, A. K., *Dynamic Facets of Indian Thought,* Vol. IV, South Asian Publishers, New Delhi, 1988.

Sarkar, S., *Towards Marx,* Papyrus, Calcutta, 1983.

Sivananda, S., *Religious Education,* The Divine Life Society, India, 1983.

Shaffer, J. A., *Philosophy of Mind*, Prentice Hall of India Private Limited, New Delhi, 1982.

Sharma, C. D., *A Critical Survey of Indian Philosophy,* Motilal Banarasidass, Delhi, 1964.

Sommervell, D. C. (abridged), *A Study of History by Arnold Toynbee,* Vol. I, Dell Publishing Co. Inc, New York, 1978.

Srivastava, R. S., *Contemporary Indian Philosophy,* Munshi Ram Manohar Lal, Delhi, 1965.

Slater, R. L., *World Religions and World Community,* Columbia University, Columbia, 1963.

Strawson, P. F., *Individuals: An Essay in Descriptive Metaphysics,* University Paperbacks, Methuen, London, 1977.

Tarkunde, V. M., *Radical Humanism, The Philosophy of Freedom and Democracy,* Ajanta Publishers, Delhi, 1983.

Tagore, R. N., *The Religion of Man,* Unwin Books, London, 1970.

Taylor, A. E., *Elements of Metaphysics,* University Paperback, Methuen London, 1961.

Tilak, B. G., *Gita Rahasya,* Tilak Brothers, Poona, 1971.

Varma, V. P., *Philosophical Humanism and Contemporary India,* Motilal Banarasidass, Delhi, 1979.

Webb, C. C. J., *Divine Personality and Human Life*, George Allen & Unwin, London, 1920.

Widgery, A. C., *The Comparative Study of Religions,* Williams & Norgate, London, 1923.

Edited Works

In Bengali

Basu, N. S., *Saswata Vivekananda,* Ananda Publishers Private Limited, Calcutta, 1992.

Chattopadhyay, B., *Sri Chaitanya Charitamrita by Krishnadas Kaviraj Goswami,* Vedavyasa Vandar, Calcutta, 1303 B. S.

Lokeswarananda, *S.,* and Others, *Chintanayak Vivekananda,* The Ramakrishna Mission Institute of Culture, Calcutta, 1384 B. S.

Sengupta, S. P., *Vivekananda Smriti,* Calcutta Book House, Calcutta, 1964.

In English

Bhajananda, S. and Mahabodhananda, S., (Ed.), *The Universal Message of Swami Vivekananda*, Ramakrishna Mission, Belur Math, Howrah, W.B, 1st. Edn. January, 2016.

Basham, A. L., *A Cultural History of India,* Oxford University Press, New Delhi,1983.

Ferm, V., *An Encyclopedia of Religion,* Philosophical Library, New York, 1945.

Guha, B. and Others, *Vivekananda Commemoration Volume,* The University of Burdwan, 1966.

Gupta, H.C. (Tr.), *Swami Vivekanada Studies in Soviet Union,* The Ramakrishna Mission Institute of Culture, Calcutta 1987.

Konstantinov, F. V. and Others, *The Fundamentals of Marxist Leninist Philosophy,* Progress Publishers, Moscow, 1982.

Lokeswarananda, S., and Others, *World Thinkers on Ramakrishna Vivekananda,* The Ramakrishna Mission Institute of Culture, Calcutta, 1983.

Loetscher, L. A., *The New Schaff-Herzog Encyclopedia of Religious Knowledge,* Baker Book House, Michigan, 1955.

Majumdar, R. C., *Vivekananda Centenary Memorial Volume,* Calcutta, 1963.

Ryazanskaya, S., *The German Ideology - Karl Marx and Frederic Engels,* Moscow, 1964.

Saint-Hilaire, P. B., *The Future Evolution of Man,* Sri Aurobindo Ashram, Pondicherry, 1974.

The Cultural Heritage of *India,* Vol. IV. The Ramakrishna Mission Institute of Culture, Calcutta, 1970.

Journals and Souvenirs

Smarak Grantha, Dumdum Vidyut Chakra Pathagar, 1972.

Udbodhan, 1368-69 B. S.

Bengalee, The 6th to 9th July, 1902.

Bulletins of Ramakrishna Mission Institute of Culture, July to Nov. 1978.

Commemorative Number, 54th Foundation Day Aniversary of the Institute Feb, 1992.

Chicago Evening Journal, Sept. 29, 1983.

Detroit Evening News, March 16, 1894.

Detroit Journal, February 16, 1894.

Detroit Free Press, Feb-April, 1894.

New York Daily Tribune, May and December, 1894. *New York Herald,* Oct 1, 1893, Jan 19, 1894.

Prabuddha Bharata, Golden Jubilee November, 1945, May, 1963, July, 1932, 1961,1963.

Vedanta Kesari, January and April, 1961.

Vedanta of the West, Nos. III-117, 119, 121,126-131, 134, 135, 158, 159.

Vivekananda Commemoration Volume, The University of Burdwan, 1966. *Washington Post,* October 29, 1894.

Index